Living
with
DOGS

Living *with* DOGS

Collecting and Traditions, At Home and Afield

TEXT BY LAURENCE SHEEHAN
PHOTOGRAPHS BY WILLIAM STITES
with Carol Sama Sheehan and Kathryn George Precourt

Clarkson Potter/Publishers
New York

Published by Clarkson N. Potter, Inc., 201 East 50th Street, New York, New York 10022.
Member of the Crown Publishing Group.
Random House, Inc. New York, Toronto, London, Sydney, Auckland
www.randomhouse.com

CLARKSON N. POTTER, POTTER, and colophon are trademarks of Clarkson N. Potter, Inc.

Printed in China

Design by Donna Agajanian

Library of Congress Cataloging-in-Publication Data
Sheehan, Laurence.
    Living with dogs / Text by Laurence Sheehan with Carol Sama Sheehan and
        Kathryn George Precourt; photographs by William Stites. — 1st ed.
    Includes index.
    1. Dogs—United States. 2. Dogs—United States—Pictorial works. I. Sheehan,
        Carol Sama. II. Precourt, Kathryn George. III. Title.
SF426.2.S535   1999
636.7'00973—dc21   98-27192

ISBN 0-517-70875-2

10   9   8   7   6   5

To all the dogs who have made a difference in our lives:

*Buttons, Maggie, Mollie, Mr. Magoo, Coodles,
Buddy, Zorro, Blue, Addie, and Buster;*

*Sarge, Baby, Muggs, Princess, Harry, Bess,
Seymour, and Hildegarde;*

*Skeeter, Robbie, Gayla, Bunnie, Betsy, Alice, Rose, Iddy Bit,
Dolly, Juno, Jake, Pumpkin, and Allegra;*

and also to Sparkle.

Contents

3 *Dogs in the Country*

4 *Dogs at Rest* 205

Introduction

When my wife, Carol, and I moved to a small town in rural western Massachusetts a few years ago, we decided it was time to get a dog. After all, with the recent ascendency of dogs in American life, statistics showed that more U.S. households—almost 40 percent—had canines than had children. Our own household felt a bit empty and quiet and neat and clean. A pooch could change all that! Of the roughly 58 million dogs in the nation, representing more than 200 breeds, surely there was one dog out there that could wear a tag with our name on it.

Actually we had both grown up with dogs in our families—Carol with beagles—Maggie, Molly, and Mr. Magoo—in Houston, and I with a succession of collie mixes and other mutts in the suburbs of New Haven, Connecticut. Later, when raising my own family, I had acquired—for the sake of the kids, you understand—an exuberant Labrador retriever mix named Blue and a purebred tricolor (black, brown, and white) collie named Zorro.

There was nothing particularly noteworthy about any of those dogs, except perhaps for the tricolor. He was a descendant of one of the Hollywood Lassies, but unfortunately he was as slow-witted as he was beautiful. A collie critic once told me that Zorro's brain capacity had been sacrificed through selective breeding for a longer snout. After hearing those harsh words, we loved Zorro even more.

Carol's and my experience growing up with dogs was probably typical of most Americans coming of age with dogs in the 1940s and 1950s. They were in our hearts and in our annual Christmas card photographs, but they were hardly the stuff of legend or obsession. Nevertheless, these many years later we decided the time had come to bring home a new dog, a leash, and maybe some flea powder. With plenty of open fields and woods surrounding our new residence, it seemed almost criminal not to have a dog. So when we came upon a litter of Australian shepherds for sale at the annual agricultural fair in a neighboring town, we took the plunge.

To our amazement, the puppy we picked out—a female who at that early stage of growth looked more like a California sea otter than a dog—radically changed our lives, and not just because of the practical impact she had on our daily routines. Addie, as we named her, made all the demands on our time and patience that any puppy new to a household does. Neither of us was prepared for the emotional impact the dog would have on us, however.

Actually, that is a lie. I had been a sucker for dogs all my life. I just never expected owning a dog would be so much like parenting. It struck me that a dramatic change had occurred over the years in the way people relate to dogs. "More people are treating their dogs as human now," animal behaviorist Peter Borchelt has observed. "There is more empathy and care for them."

Carol developed a kind of sympathetic hypochondria on behalf of our young dog. By subscribing to a couple of newsletters published by eminent veterinary schools, she learned about an astonishing range of maladies and disorders to which dogs are susceptible. Routine trips to the vet gave her the opportunity to air all her concerns with bat-

teries of questions: What do we do if Addie gets a fever? Is it all right for her to eat people food? Will she get cancer if she chews on firewood?

I turned into my own worst nightmare—a guy who carries a picture of his dog around with him in his wallet. I woke up in the morning dreamily contemplating the image of Addie's face. My clothes came back from the cleaners with Milk-Bone crumbs pressed into the fabric. I worried ceaselessly, not that Addie would contract some bizarre canine disease, but that she would be hit by a car, like my first dog, Coodles.

Coming home after being away on a trip for a couple of days, I would get so excited about seeing Addie again that I would practically knock Carol over on my way to the dog. And I came bearing gifts: new latex toys, rawhide chews, hambone-scented Frisbees, boxes of a snack advertised as "the treats dogs go jerky for." Of course, I was the one going jerky.

In time, our irrational worries subsided, Addie entered fully into our lives, and like all other dog owners these days, we studied up on her heritage. Australian shepherds are best known for herding sheep. The breed originated in the Basque country of Spain and France and came to the American West as a herding dog by way of Australia in the late 1800s. We had named Addie for the city of Adelaide, Down Under, but it turns out that Biarritz and Denver would have been fitting names, too.

Today's dog-owning culture is in fact characterized by a fascination with the history and evolution of people's favorite breeds. More purebreds are registered with the American Kennel Club than ever before, and their popularity has spawned a revival in traditional dog portraiture and an explosion in contemporary dog photography, some of which is of very high caliber. Pride of breed has propelled many dog owners to collect anything and everything that bears the image of their dogs, from inexpensive porcelain figurines to priceless bronzes and oils. When Sotheby's in New York auctioned off the Duke and Duchess of Windsor's collection of pug figurines, pug owners from all over the country descended on the auc-

tion house. Some of them carried their own live pugs in their arms, while a few wore slippers embroidered with pugs, perhaps to bring them good luck in the bidding.

Every breed of dog seems to come with its own constellation of fact and fancy, a kind of anecdotal history breathing life into the dry profile of the official breed standard. Pug owners, for example, are likely to regale any willing listener with the story of the pug that bit Napoleon when he climbed into the imperial bed on his wedding night or with the fact that pugs kept Mary Queen of Scots company on her way to her execution for treason.

Canis familiaris has been a part of art, literature, and legend almost from the time it was first domesticated some 10,000 years ago. From Cerberus, the three-headed hound that guards the gates of hell in Greek mythology, to Snoopy, the philosophical beagle of the comic strip "Peanuts," dogs have played an amazing variety of roles in our imagination and in our popular culture. Mere background figures in medieval and Renaissance paintings, dogs became central figures in canvases painted for English and European aristocrats beginning in the 18th century. As early as 1700, porcelain and pottery were adorned with dog images or fashioned in the shape of dogs. Practical canine accessories such as leashes and col-

lars were also richly ornamented in tribute to the dog and as a display of the owner's wealth. In the 20th century, dogs became a popular motif in advertising and promotion, and Hollywood struck it rich with dozens of movies featuring the canine superstars Rin-Tin-Tin and Lassie. It did not take long for dogs to break into television, either.

Cultural references like these help to bestow both romance and gravitas on a beloved breed, perhaps turning a dog's inherent shortcomings into virtues, and allow dog owners, if they are so inclined, to endow their dogs of choice with historical cachet. Try as one may, one cannot do this for pets like parakeets, gerbils, or even cats. (To steal a line from James Thurber, "There is no deliberate intention here to offend admirers of the cat, although I don't really much care whether I do or not.") Save their purported masters, dogs support narrative better than any other living thing.

Take English setters. A couple of years after we obtained Addie, I came upon a dog named Buster in a kennel at a veterinary clinic. Buster, a healthy two-year-old English setter, was a casualty of divorce and was sorely in need of a new home. Apart from vaguely understanding that setters were bird dogs, I had not a clue about the nature of this particular breed. Yet when Buster stared up at me with his liquid brown eyes, tail wagging furiously, the sight of him gave me pause. His upper lip was hung up on one side of his freckled muzzle and one ear was flopped, pink side out, giving him a slightly deranged, ready-for-anything aspect. I was hooked.

Unfortunately, when I got Buster home I realized that Carol, Addie, and Emma, our calico cat, were not as ready for anything as Buster was. Briefly we became a dysfunctional family as I struggled with a willful, free-spirited dog who was deaf to the command "Come!"

Training dogs requires patience, firmness, and a steady dispensation of positive reinforcement. Not only does a good trainer take into account the behaviorial traits and instincts of the breed, but he or she must also consider the unique personality of the individual dog. To me, Buster was E. B. White's dachshund, Fred, made over.

"When I address Fred I never have to raise either my voice or my hopes," White wrote, in *Harper's,* about the folly of trying to train Fred. "He even disobeys me when I instruct him in something that he wants to do."

Buster spent most of that first summer disobeying me

and getting into trouble—skirmishing with porcupines and skunks, running after large trucks, burying himself alive under a neighbor's utility building (we had to chainsaw through the floor to get him out). The more I learned about English setters, however, the less flummoxed I became with Buster's behavior. "There's a unique disorder to these dogs," observed one of my neighbors, a lifelong bird hunter who knew setters well. "Each one always seems to come with some little quirk." Others familiar with the breed told of setters that ate rocks, leaped off cliffs, or ran headlong into trees. Some techniques used to bridle a setter's natural exuberance would draw charges of animal abuse today. To keep his setter from running into the next county, one hunter I talked to weighed the dog down with a 15-pound chain around the neck. Another actually tied one foreleg to his dog's collar, effectively turning the dog into a more manageable three-legged setter in the field.

I came to my senses about Buster when it dawned on me that an English setter had been the model for that classic Disney vehicle of ditzy dumbness, Goofy. This realization somehow made it easier to accept Buster for what he was—an animal with attention deficit disorder by day, a lovesick couch potato by night. In the weeks and months that followed that breakthrough in understanding, we all settled into a much more predictable and agreeable routine around the house.

I gave up trying to be the alpha dog and settled for something that might be called passive mastery. By letting Buster run free several mornings a week, when traffic was almost nonexistent, I gave the dog back his enjoyment of liberty. He in turn more graciously embraced his terms of confinement inside the house, under the disdainful scrutiny of Addie and Emma, along with his periods of controlled recess, tied to a forgivingly long lead in the middle of the hayfield with bones, sticks, kangaroo mice, and butterflies at hand to entertain him. An intricate system of checks and balances fell into place in the household: Addie slept upstairs, Buster took the love seat in the living room, and Emma . . . Well, we were never really sure where the cat went at night, but we were fairly certain that Buster ceased to get on her nerves.

Anyway, peace came slowly. The secret of living with dogs is to take the wild with the sweet, and then sit back and wait for the laughs and the love. "Dogs are not our whole life," Roger Caras, author and president of the ASPCA, wisely observes, "but they make our lives whole."

PART ONE

At Home with DOGS

Virginia Woolf seems to have written *Flush*, her "biography" of a spaniel once owned by the poet Elizabeth Barrett Browning, largely as a lark, but in one early passage she managed to render the quintessential English model for dogs in the home:

"Between them lay the widest gulf that can separate one being from another. She spoke. He was dumb. She was woman; he was

Above and opposite: **In the homes of dog lovers like Virginia Keresey, a canine collection may be limited in scope, in this case to antique dog collars, but it is invariably rounded out with other acquisitions, such as old and new books on dogs. The rare bronze mastiff's head over the mantel, dating from ancient Roman times but affectionately known as Bob, originally came off the bow of a ship.**

dog. Thus closely united, thus immensely divided, they gazed at each other. Then with one bound Flush sprang on to the sofa and laid himself where he was to lie for ever after—on the rug at Miss Barrett's feet."

That scene was set in the mid-19th century, but it would take at least a hundred more years for dogs in America to achieve the exalted domestic status of Flush. In 1900 few dogs were even allowed in households in this country. Dogs bred for sport were kept in kennels. Herding dogs lived with their flocks. Farm dogs lived in barns or in doghouses nailed together out of scrap lumber. After dogs became more common as family pets in the prosperous years following World War II, they were still largely relegated to backyards and makeshift outdoor quarters. But upscale sporting goods stores like Abercrombie & Fitch, as early as the 1940s, recognized that dogs were acquiring considerable cachet among their upwardly mobile customers.

"Blue ribbon entry or family pet, your dog comes into his own at A. & F.," read a catalog published for the Madison Avenue, New York, emporium in 1942. "Throughout the store, you'll find gifts and gadgets for dogs and dog lovers. We make to your personal order show prizes, jewelry, ornaments, and home accessories designed around the dog motif."

The canine race began to make inroads not just in stores but in hearth and home as well, first infiltrating the kitchen, then making incursions on the den, and by the 1990s even storming our bedrooms.

"What's the point of having a twelve-pound dog if it doesn't sleep with you?" asks Ann Patchett, a novelist living in Nashville, in a column in *Vogue* on the subject of her passion for Rose, an abandoned terrier mix she rescued in a city park. The column sparked enthusiastic fan mail, including a note from a thirty-eight-year-old woman with two Yorkshire terriers. "There isn't an $8,000 gown in the world," wrote the owner of the Yorkies, in pointed reference to one of the icons of *Vogue*-style glamour, "that can lower your stress, make you laugh, give you love, cover your face with wet kisses, or keep you warm like a dog can."

The depth of affection and gratitude many dog owners feel for their pets can be seen in the freedom they accord the creatures within the house. Dogs bred and trained not primarily for companionship but for hunting, herding, or guarding generally never see the inside of a private residence, but it is another matter if the dog is a pet. Some owners give their dogs the run of the house, while others draw the line at certain rooms. The size of the dog does not seem to be a consideration in allocating favors. Great Danes and Bernese mountain dogs are as likely to be granted unrestricted movement in a home as are Pekes and Poms—the diminutive Pekingese and Pomeranians one expects to see curled up on pillows or ottomans.

Most dog trainers advocate teaching dogs, no matter how small or large, to stay off the furniture, but that advice is ignored by owners from what might be called the Slipcover School of Dog Management. These folks, using slipcovers and throws to protect their finer pieces, can't bring themselves to deny their pets the soft comforts they themselves enjoy. Coming home to a dog in the window or at the

Above and opposite: **While some dog fanciers invest heavily in canine accoutrements for the home, Kathryn and Geoffrey Precourt used inexpensive flea-market finds to pay homage to the dog in the kitchen of their country house.**
Above right: **Fine dog paintings emerged as an art form in the 18th century, beginning with commissions to depict sporting dogs and hounds in action, as these terriers in pursuit of varmints, probably badgers.**

door, especially one filled with joy at the very sight of you, seems to make up for any wear and tear the animals may inflict on the premises. People who own large dogs with long tails quickly learn to keep their crystal vases off low tables. Owners whose dogs come in and out of the house in all kinds of weather learn to keep towels handy by the door.

In fact, dogs settle into a home pretty much the way people do, gravitating to a favorite corner, window, or chair. Like children, they leave their toys scattered around—a rubber squeaky here or a half-gnawed bone there. These objects, along with the leashes, collars, food bowls, dog beds, and all the other paraphernalia associated with keeping a dog, turn a house into a habitat—and, late at night when all the lights are out, a minefield. When dog owners add dog art and collectibles to their decor, whether specific to their favorite breed or in praise of dogs in general, the habitat becomes a gallery.

"Home is where the dog is," writes Marjorie Garber, the author of *Dog Love,* in explanation of the rise in popularity of canine iconography and of the ability of dogs to insinuate themselves into the homes of all kinds of people. "The puppy represents what the yuppie fantasizes about childhood, what the older person fantasizes about youth, what the city-dweller fantasizes about the country, what the weary workaholic fantasizes about freedom, what the human spouse or partner fantasizes about spontaneity, emotional generosity, and togetherness. In soft-focus television commercials, and at the front door, the dog, leash patiently in mouth, is always waiting for you."

DOGGED COLLECTORS

A single yellow dog food bowl, made by an American potter in the 1940s and inscribed "Man's Best Friend," rapidly expanded into a collection of objects that gives a jaunty canine stamp to a New York apartment and a country house in the hills of western Massachusetts.

Lifelong collectors of antiques of all kinds, and habitués of flea markets and antiques shops wherever they travel, Kathryn and Geoffrey Precourt were naturally drawn to canine artifacts. Both had grown up with dogs, Kathryn with Scotties, Geoffrey with schnauzers.

Actually, as very young children, Geoffrey and his brother, Harry, had to persuade their parents some before obtaining their first dog. Every December the boys would request a dog for Christmas.

Right: **Study of a spaniel, oil on canvas in a tramp art frame, greets visitors in the entry hall of the Precourts' country house** *(above),* **along with a dog doorbell from the local flea market. Under the peg rack, used for stowing leashes of several lengths for the couple's terriers, is a reproduction Scottie doorstop and a metal Lab once used as the nameplate for a mailbox.**

"You can't have a dog this year. What else would you like?" asked their parents.

"A leash," replied the boys.

"No!"

"Then how about a dog bowl?"

Years later, when Geoffrey and Kathryn were newly married, they planned to adopt a dog they could both call their own. They bought another distinguished food dish just a week after they found that first yellow one. "We now had something in which to serve a dog both food and water," Kathryn notes. "We even had picked out a name—Seymour. So it was about time to pick out the dog."

Below: **Pillows were fashioned by Gracie Wilkins for the Precourts out of scraps of old fabric with humorous canine silhouettes and messages, such as "Good Dog" and "Woof."** *Right:* **A valuable tabletop collection of inkwells is guarded by a milk glass dog, a common mantel ornament in Victorian England.**

Opposite, above: **Geoffrey Precourt relaxes with his Dandie Dinmont, Seymour, in a newly built country house filled with the ambience of its collections, canine and otherwise.**

Below: **The random collection of comical French dog dishes, some made to order for B. Altman & Co., includes a universal dog fantasy, here depicted by a dachshund dreaming about steak.**

After dipping into the many dog books, old and new, they had acquired, and consulting the American Kennel Club's Web site describing the virtues of purebred dogs of all kinds, the Precourts narrowed the choices down to two breeds: the petit basset griffon Vendéen, a raggedy-looking but perky French hunting dog bred to track rabbits and other small prey, and the Dandie Dinmont terrier, a coal-eyed little dog with a witty, independent streak, also a hunter of diminutive varmints. Both breeds met the Precourts' main requirements for a dog—that it behave well with children, that it feel equally at home in city and country, and that it weigh 25 pounds or less—the limit imposed on dogs traveling with passengers on Metro North, the rail service that provides the Precourts' link between city and country.

"But we didn't really make up our minds between the two breeds until we ran into a fellow walking his Dandie one Christmas season in front of Saint Patrick's Cathedral," recalls Geoffrey. "The dog was such a pleasure to watch and to interact with that we decided, then and there, it was for us. We contacted its breeder in Virginia and got on the waiting list for a puppy."

Within months, Seymour walked—make that scurried at high speed—into their lives, "and at this point we have antique dog things in every room of the house," says Kathryn. Special occasions came along to further expand their collection. Geoffrey bought Kathryn an old oil portrait of a Scottish terrier for her birthday, Scotties being the dogs of her youth. Kathryn commissioned photographer Mary Schjeldahl to shoot a portrait of Seymour as a Valentine's Day gift for Geoffrey. An ivory stickpin with the carved likeness of a Clumber spaniel, for her, was matched by a set of shirt studs in the image of bird dogs, for him. When Kathryn came upon a set of genial dog prints by Diana Thorne, a children's book illustrator of the 1930s, she knew she had the perfect artwork to embellish the walls of the children's guest room in the country house.

"Generally, we look for images of dogs that have personality and are friendly, not mean," says Kathryn. "Many dog owners only collect what is specific to the breed or breeds that they happen to own or care about the most," Kathryn points out. "But we've enjoyed collecting across the board. Our first rule is 'Buy what you like,' but searching for that special thing is part of the fun."

One breed-specific item the couple did collect was a pitcher advertising a short-lived, allegedly undrinkable product called Dandee Dinmont Scotch. "It's not valuable, but it makes a good vase for country flowers," notes Kathryn Precourt. A lithograph of an American Staffordshire terrier called Nip was just as interesting to them, as was a charcoal study of a Newfoundland with

Above: **In a guest bedroom fitted out for dog people, there are Airedale terriers, soft and hard,
and a 19th-century print of puppies by Currier & Ives.** *Left:* **The bedroom dresser is arrayed in canine miscellany,
including an old electric-light perfume scenter and a new hand puppet from The Nature Company.**

traditional brass collar, in a frame with a border made out of the chain from a dog's leash. The couple also collect tramp art picture frames, well suited to dog images.

Seymour joined the Precourts on excursions to the flea market every Sunday, accepting biscuits from any dealer who would proffer them. But it wasn't long before he lost interest in antiques. Sophie, a West Highland white terrier on another floor in his building, had caught his eye. "They hit it off from day one," reports Kathryn. "We now arrange 'play dates' for them. Everybody in the building knows they are an item. Where will it end?"

Right: **The guest bathroom carries on the canine motif with a Majolica plate painted with an English sheepdog, a watercolor of a beagle, and a Victorian lustreware mug with the image of a guard dog.**
Opposite: **Prints by the 1930s children's book illustrator Diana Thorne were framed and hung in the bunk room to make it more kid friendly for the likes of Emily Worcester, daughter of a neighbor, and Addie, an Australian shepherd.**

BREEDER'S CHOICE

When Cathy Nelson returned from a rugged three-week safari in Kenya and Tanzania, during which she and her party tracked the daily routines of elephants, rhinos, giraffes, cheetahs, hyenas, and assorted other wild beasts of Africa, a friend asked her how she had held up under the stress and strain of the travel.

"Oh, I had no problems at all," she replied. "I'm not bragging, you know. It's just that I have a dog show constitution."

For more than three decades, Cathy and her husband, John, have bred and trained Dandie Dinmont terriers, which they have shown in dog show rings across the country. "The gentleman among the terriers," as she describes the breed, "cherished for its compatibility with young families as well as its independent personality."

Traveling twenty to thirty weekends in some years from her home

Above: **Cathy Nelson has been breeding Dandie Dinmonts, "the gentlemen among terriers," for more than three decades.** *Right:* **A vitrine in the Nelson house displays badges of success that Cathy's top dogs have earned in competition over the years.**

base in Potomac, Maryland, and routinely putting tens of thousands of miles on her Chrysler minivan, Nelson has learned firsthand the rigors of campaigning her dogs on the show circuit. Once, before a show in suburban Cleveland, car trouble forced her to groom the dogs outside a gas station, unplugging its Coke machine so she could use her hair dryer to fluff up the animals. Another time, having prepared homemade vichyssoise to serve to sixty judges and stewards at an important dog club luncheon near her home, Cathy inadvertently left the house with refrigerated containers of puppy formula instead of the soup. When she got to the luncheon and saw no scallions floating in the contents of her containers, she called home, only to be told, "The puppies didn't like their breakfast."

Unlike many owners, Cathy made her job harder but, she says, more satisfying, by grooming and showing her dogs herself instead of hiring a professional handler. "Some people are happy to be checkbook owners, but I enjoy the travel, the socializing, and most of all the competition," she says. She also learned a lot about showing dogs by watching other handlers in the ring. "Purebreds are judged against a standard that is a word picture of the ideal in each breed, but no dog is perfect and judging itself is necessarily subjective," she explains. "The job of handlers is to hide a dog's faults and highlight its virtues, without making themselves conspicuous. The best handlers don't even look as if they are moving. Myself, I fuss too much. I've seen

Above left: **Above littermates Theda and Ford, the 1889 oil painting** *Yorkshire Dandies* **by Lucy Waller portrays the terriers of Ainsty Kennel going to ground in the English countryside.** *Above right:* **The Nelson library, an example of single-breed collecting, is a cornucopia of Dandie Dinmont books, artifacts, and memorabilia.**

myself on videotape in the ring looking like a flock of starlings, I'm so busy."

Nevertheless, Cathy's efforts have paid off handsomely, as in 1993, when Butler, in his final ring appearance before retirement, won the Terrier Group at New York's Westminster Kennel Club show, the World Series of canine events.

"But there are also years when things don't work out for your dogs," Cathy observes. One dog she showed never did well at outdoor shows after it had rained. "She hated wet grass and would walk as if on eggs, with a horrid mincing gait that the judges invariably marked her down for." In truth, Cathy says she gets as much pleasure from placing puppies with good families as she does from winning titles. "If you're in it just for the ribbons, you won't do it long."

When the Nelsons acquired their first Dandie, Ruffles, as a pet, Cathy was working as a freelance illustrator of children's books in the Chicago area. Meeting other breeders and owners of Dandies whetted her interest in the breed, and soon she was raising them herself. Her interest in art inspired her to collect images of Dandies, and today her house in suburban Maryland boasts tributes to the breed in oil, silver, porcelain, paper, and bronze. "I'm not partial to one medium or another, as some collectors are, but I do concentrate on the single breed. Art depicting Dandies is hard to find, simply because the dogs themselves are rare, so when I come upon something I really like, I jump on it."

Above: **Newborn Dandies rest in their kennel in the Nelson den.**
Below, left and right: **Portraits of Dandies by Maud Earl and Graham Roe, both dating from about the turn of the century, invest the Nelson living room and dining room with the regal image of a small dog who would be king.**

LAKESIDE KENNELS

From a breeding program that began in 1936, when Robert Wehle (pronounced Way-lee), then only sixteen, mated smart, quick Gem of Fearn to strong, docile Frank of Sunnylawn, the pointers of his Elhew Kennels have developed into what sporting authority Tom Davis calls "the Purdey, the Lafite-Rothschild, the Lamborghini of bird dogs." The dogs of Elhew Kennels in Henderson, New York, and Midway, Alabama, have been winning field trial championships on every species of game bird with almost monotonous regularity for more than forty years. Hunters prize the Elhew pointers as gun dogs.

The kennels in Henderson are part of a sprawling peaceable kingdom that Wehle has created for himself and his wife, Gatra, atop the limestone cliffs overlooking Lake Ontario. Brightly feathered guinea

Above: **Pointer breeder Robert Wehle shows off Snakefoot, the pride of Elhew Kennels, named Top Shooting Dog of the Year in 1994–95.** *Right:* **A pointer portrait gallery graces the kennel in Henderson, New York, where collars, leashes, training whistles, and other supplies are stored.**

hens, jungle fowl, and fighting cocks strut free on the lawns and among a patchwork of lush flower and vegetable gardens, giving a wide berth to any visitor. In the evenings, whitetail deer and wild turkeys appear and feed on a smorgasbord of seeds and grains left for them at selected locations. A herd of long-haired Scottish cattle, raised here primarily for fun, offer their shaggy profiles in a pasture set against the slate-colored vastness of the lake.

Perched above the lake is a blue-shuttered limestone house where Bob and Gatra live in the summer months. Underfoot are two Alabama-born rat terriers named Barnum and Bailey, who are a bit overweight from being lavished with table scraps. They follow Gatra wherever she goes, in or out. The house, a nearby guest cottage, and a studio where Wehle sculpts animal and human figures for casting in bronze, are all adorned with images of dogs, birds, horses, and other creatures. Tables sag under back issues of the *Pointing Dog Journal* and *Shooting Sportsman,* and when the phone rings, it is often someone hoping to obtain a pup from the latest Elhew litter.

"We don't want our dogs to experience any kind of pain, discomfort, or fear," Wehle says as he gives a visitor a tour of the grounds. His benign approach to bringing up dogs permeates the two classic bird dog training books he has written, *Wing and Shot,* and *Snakefoot, the Making of a Champion,* and it is even more apparent in his affection for every dog in his kennel, from puppy to champion. A strongly built

Below: **The Wehle house is filled with country antiques and artistic tributes to pointers and other animals.** *Opposite, above:* **Barnum and Bailey, rat terriers from Alabama, follow Gatra wherever she goes; the Wehles freely admit to spoiling their house dogs.** *Below:* **Puppies are handled, fussed over, and sweet-talked from the day they are whelped. Wehle maintains that such treatment, "influencing and molding rather than intimidating and forcing," is the foundation for successful training later on.**

man and commanding figure, now in his seventies, Bob speaks to each dog by name as he walks along a line of outdoor runs. He slips each dog a liver treat from the pocket of his safari jacket. "Ideally, throughout a young dog's life," he remarks, "it should be uninhibited, gregarious, and full of confidence."

That applies most suitably to a particularly sturdy and keen-looking pointer whom Bob introduces as Snakefoot, "the finest dog I've ever raised." Now retired to stud after an exemplary career on the field trial circuit, Snakefoot commands the highest stud fee ever put on a pointer: $1,500.

In the run next to Snakefoot is Discovery, one of Snakefoot's progeny. "He is a one-year-old tornado," Wehle says admiringly. Some 150 pointer puppies are born at the kennel every year. The velvet-glove treatment starts in a whelping shed, the temporary home to females who have been bred to Snakefoot and other precocious males. The birthing chamber is even equipped with an incubator that Wehle obtained from a human hospital.

Bob decides to take out two four-month-old puppies for a training session. Walking the puppies on grassy paths through the woods, without collar or lead, he explains, is a socialization technique designed to win the dogs' hearts and to hone their pointing instincts. He carries a long stick with a string attached to it, a pheasant wing dangling from the string. Once in a while he casts the wing into the light

brush near one of the dogs. Presented with the wing, the dogs go stock still, and Wehle then lays hands on them to reinforce the desirable pointing stance.

Arriving at a shed called a recall pen, Bob releases a flurry of farm-raised quail. The birds scatter in all directions, and the puppies bound after them. "The birds happen to be moulting now, so they are slow," he notes, "but in another few weeks they'll flush like rockets." He goes on to explain that it is slightly risky to expose the puppies to birds that are losing their feathers and are therefore unable to get away with their usual dispatch. He does not want to teach the young dogs to actually catch birds, just to point to where they are, for the waiting hunter.

After a while, Wehle sets his training stick on the ground to give the brown-and-white puppy an affectionate massage. "Aren't you beautiful? Aren't you wonderful?" he croons in a deep, melodious voice. The black-and-white puppy picks up the pheasant wing in his teeth and runs off with it, dragging the long stick attached to it awkwardly behind him. "Pa-up—ho!" Bob cries, trudging slowly in the direction of the runaway. "Such tenacity," he states, admiringly.

Finally Bob recovers the stick and turns homeward. The puppies dart in and out of the woods ahead of him. "They're doing just fine," he says, nodding with satisfaction. When he gets back to the kennels, Snakefoot, Discovery, and dozens of the other pointers head for the fences and break into a full-throated chorus of welcome for their undisputed master.

Left: **In his studio** *(below)*, **Bob Wehle sculpts pointers and other animals in clay and bronze.** *Center left:* **Marksman, an outstanding pointer from the 1950s, is buried on the kennel grounds.** *Bottom left:* **A pointer skeleton is a useful reference in a kennel room used for checking on the health and condition of the dogs.**

Opposite: **Elhew Kennels has produced thousands of pointer puppies over the past six decades; their achievements are recorded in word and image in house and kennel.**

ARTFUL RESTRAINTS

Throughout the centuries, dog owners have used collars, humble and patrician, to restrain, identify, and coddle their animals, whether fierce dogs of the hunt or the precious lap companions of Victorian England. They are seen adorning dogs in ancient Egyptian and Roman wall paintings and in tapestries from the Middle Ages.

For Virginia Keresey, these artful restraints have uncommon resonance, and for more than two decades she has built a collection of more than three hundred dog collars, which are scattered throughout her New York City apartment. Some are simple, others ornately decorated with semiprecious stones, and they attest to supreme craftsmanship in leather, brass, iron, and silver. She occasionally wears some of the more delicate collars as necklaces or bracelets. But apart from

Above: **One of the antique collars collected by Virginia Keresey, atop an 18th-century Spanish writing box, has a cow's head in copper, suggesting it was made to go around the neck of a butcher's dog.**
Right: **An English oil painting of a greyhound hangs over an English Regency desk bristling with finely crafted dog collars of silver, gold, and bronze, and two 19th-century silver dog combs, "the ultimate froufrou," observes their present owner.**

their appeal as works of art, each collar has a story to tell, and each story illuminates the history of the relationship between humans and dogs.

Keresey, a great-niece of the noted collector and dog fancier Mabel Brady Garvan, attributes her interest in collecting collars to her childhood love of animals. "Horses and dogs have been part of my life since I was very young," she explains. "My parents have told me that even at four years of age I was fitting my dog and all the other dogs in the neighborhood with collars made of ribbons and sashes."

The most notable dog in Mrs. Garvan's Dungarvan Kennels was undoubtedly Champion My Own Brucie, a cocker spaniel, "one of the greatest specimens ever produced in this country both as a show dog and a sire," read the animal's obituary in the *New York Times* in 1943. Bred by Herman E. Mellenthin of Poughkeepsie, New York, Brucie won best in show at Morris and Essex, then the world's largest dog show, having an entry of 4,456, and followed that up with two consecutive victories at Westminster.

The most poignant collars in the Keresey collection today are those that reflect the heroic behavior that dogs have exhibited in behalf of their masters. Collars that belonged to mascots, World War II messenger dogs, Red Cross dogs, and St. Bernards, for example, all reflect an individual dog's single-minded devotion to a higher purpose.

Opposite: **Silver dog collars with central medallions made by W. H. Haseler Ltd., Birmingham, England, one of them inscribed to a greyhound, Swivel Link, for winning a 500-yard race at Wimbledon in 1931.** *Below left:* **Sharp, protruding spikes on the collar at left indicate it was probably made to protect the neck of a hunting dog from bears, boars, and wolves. Above it is an 18th-century leather collar with brass studs and multiple bells, possibly Flemish.** *Below right:* **Examples of 19th-century American craftsmanship include a collar adorned with spaniels, silver plated over bronze and inscribed with the name Stevenson Crothers, and one with bulldogs in bronze relief.**

Above: **A variety of 17th- and 18th-century silver collars made in northern Holland circa 1650.** *Below:* **An ancient Roman sarcophagus panel makes a transcendent background for some of the most prized collars in Virginia Keresey's collection.** *Opposite:* **Collars of various designs lend their regal air to a 17th-century Italian chair.**

Among the rarest collars are a gilded Renaissance collar believed to be of Flemish origin, with bells and a delicately carved gargoyle to which the lead ring is attached, and a brass collar with exquisite workmanship, inscribed "IOST" and dated 1593. It is thought to be the earliest Dutch dog collar in existence. There are also collars representing the Arts and Crafts movement in England and the Tiffany tradition in America. Some of these collars bear thought-provoking inscriptions, such as the large brass collar of plain design inscribed, "Presented to the Dog 'Cromwell' by his old Shipmates S.S. 'Great Eastern,' Sheerness, 1871," or the 19th-century brass collar stating simply, "Boweds Coton Brokers Dog. Exchange."

Keresey's collection is all the more impressive considering how hard it is to locate old collars. "It's not as if there are any antique dealers specializing in collars," she says. "Many have had one or two over their years in the business, but many others say they've never seen any. The consensus is that they are very hard to find."

Keresey tries to maintain a sense of humor and whimsy in her collecting, never becoming so serious that fun and surprise are sacrificed. "I get just as much joy finding a simple leather collar belonging to someone's cherished Rover as I do discovering an important or rare piece."

In this spirit, Virginia has assembled an extensive collection of collars and memorabilia that belonged to Morris Frank.

"Frank was a blind teenager in the 1920s. When the *Saturday Evening Post* ran an article on a guide-dog program for the blind that had originated in Germany during World War I," Keresey explains, "Frank inquired about getting such a dog for himself, and he was matched with Buddy, a female German Shepherd."

In gratitude for the liberating effect Buddy's service had on him, Frank went to work for the Seeing Eye institute to foster the use of guide dogs in the United States. "He named every subsequent guide dog he had Buddy, and the publicity he received in traveling with Buddy helped pave the way for more guide dogs and for allowing blind people to enjoy life more fully."

Frank and veterinarian Dr. Mark Morris Sr. cofounded what was then known as the Buddy Foundation to underwrite research into diseases threatening the health and lives of America's companion animals. As Dr. Morris said at the time, "Pets serve as surrogate family for the elderly and countless childless couples. They are the guardians of property and human life, and they provide not only the companionship and learning for the young but unforgettable lessons in responsibility, humaneness, and gentleness." He concluded, "Their health, injuries, and illnesses are of real and lasting importance to humans." Echoing that message since 1948, the Buddy Foundation, renamed the Morris Animal Foundation, has provided $13 million to fund 650 studies to benefit animals.

"I can think of no more important or touching example of the partnership of people and dogs than the Seeing Eye dog program," Keresey observes. "Someone has to preserve the history, because this relationship has transformed the lives of blind people worldwide."

Starting with Trooper, a beagle, dogs and horses were an integral part of Ginny's youth in Oyster Bay, New York. Even in graduate school, she found time to win dog show honors for Mandy, her golden retriever. Her emotional connection with animals has also influenced her collecting impulses: "I instinctively respond to beautiful utilitarian objects that I know have been worn by man's best friend."

Opposite: **Antique canine artifacts on a desk in the living room include an 18th-century Japanese bronze foo dog, once used to burn incense, and a spiked brass collar marked, "Wm. Eckles, Island Hill, 1792." On the neck of the porcelain dog is a hallmarked silver hawk collar once used in the sport of falconry. The oil painting, dated 1881, is by American genre artist John George Brown.**

CANINE KITSCH

The jigsawed family doghouse in Betsy Speert's kitchen in suburban Boston originally hung in the dining room of the house where she and her siblings grew up in Scarsdale, New York. It was made by her uncle Herman with a lineup of movable wood terrier figures representing each member of the family.

"If someone got fresh at the dinner table," Betsy recalls, "the dog with his or her name on it went into the doghouse," adding, "Dad did the moving of the dogs."

Nowadays the miniature doghouse joins many humble canine artifacts that Betsy, an interior designer, has retrieved from flea markets and junk shops, artfully transforming her house, without breaking the bank, into a home proud of its allegiance to the image of the dog in many different forms.

Above: **A variety of bulldogs, none of special value, achieves a collective impact in Betsy Speert's dog-centered house.** *Right:* **Pictures and figurines of terriers dominate one wall, itself papered with a dog motif, in the kitchen. The Scotty sconces, found in different shops, were originally flower vases.** *Following pages:* **Betsy's living room is an inviting retreat for anyone fond of dogs.**

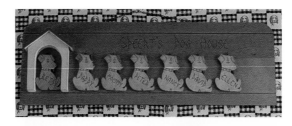

Top: **The Speert family as terriers: Betsy, Daddy, Mommy, Peter, Nancy, David, and Ellen.** *Above left:* **Speert designed her kitchen wall cabinet around a pediment she found as salvage.** *Above right:* **A Scotty lamp illuminates a terrier set piece in one corner of the kitchen; most of the dog portraits came to Betsy as gifts from her mother over the years.** *Opposite:* **Although the owner grew up with boxers, the many needlepoint pillows she has designed and made celebrate a variety of breeds. The cow paintings in the den were collected as a tribute to the Aberdeen Angus cattle that her grandparents raised.**

Terriers and bulldogs are the predominant breeds around the house. "I started collecting terriers because of a little bronze terrier Mom gave me in 1981," says Betsy, "but I really don't know why I started collecting bulldogs."

Although some of her acquisitions were serendipitous, Betsy made a conscious effort to seek out things that made sense for her 1937 Cape Cod–style house.

"The fabrics in the house, the painted furniture, and the bronzes and other artwork of dogs all have a very specific style, the 1930s look of things," she notes.

Although friends have tried to help her achieve her special look with gifts of the canine kind, the designer prefers to do her own legwork.

Adding their creature comforts to the seating in the Speert house are embroidered and needlepoint pillows with dog motifs, some of them purchased at tag sales, others made by Betsy during evenings spent listening to audiotaped books, a medium she prefers to TV. And there are artifacts bearing no relation to her affection for dogs. In a room that serves as a den, landscapes with cows—a tribute to the Aberdeen Angus cattle once raised by her grandparents—compete with the sculptures of bulldogs for attention.

HOME AWAY FROM HOME

Where else but at a camp for dogs can one learn to bake homemade liver muffins?

The founder and director of Camp Gone to the Dogs, Honey Loring, calls it Disneyland for dog nuts, but her camp epitomizes the joyous connection many dog owners have with their pets, and the sometimes admittedly silly extremes they will go to in order to reinforce that connection. A week at the camp becomes an entertaining and educational romp for both owners and dogs, with everything from serious obedience training and seminars on nutrition and disease, to frivolous doggie costume parties, bathing suit pageants, and tail-wagging contests, all set against the natural beauty of Vermont in the summer and the fall.

"The dogs have such a good time they sleep for two days after it's

Above: **Retrieving is one of many practical skills taught at Camp Gone to the Dogs in Vermont.** *Right:* **The camp combines obedience and agility trials with less serious diversions that keep both the dogs and their owners on their toes.**

over," Loring reports. "Some people even tell me their dogs get depressed for a while, they miss camp so much."

In past years, camp sessions have been held on the campuses of Putney School and Marlboro College and at the Brownsville Lodge at the base of Mount Ascutney. With over 250 dogs and their owners taking part, each week is a memorable non-stop foray into the world of canines at their sweetest and most playful. Spats between canine campers are virtually nonexistent. Maybe it's the egalitarian atmosphere: old dogs, puppies, purebreds, and designer dogs, as Loring calls mixed breeds, are all equally welcome.

"The camp gives people a chance to totally indulge themselves in their passion for dogs," says Loring, a licensed psychologist who has studied, written about, lectured on, and lived with dogs virtually all her life, her present live-ins being three standard poodles, Athena, Olympia, and Black Hawk, and an ex-racing greyhound, Joy.

Her dogs have done pet modeling—Athena was featured in the magazine spoof *Canine Quarterly*. A lifelong animal lover, Loring began grooming dogs in 1979 and went full-time into pets in 1984, when she started her own business designing and manufacturing pet products such as safety collars. Proper training of dogs increasingly has become important to her. "I really believe that a well-trained dog is

Above: **Dogs and owners relax between camp activities. One repeat camper describes the annual gathering as "a melting pot of loved and cherished pets of every size, color, and shape, where dog dreams come true."**

Above: **Puppies and mixed breeds, "one-of-a-kind designer dogs," are as welcome at camp as full-grown purebreds, but dogs with aggressive/fear problems may not fit into the program.** *Below:* **A hurdles course is one of a variety of ways in which the camp tests the agility and stamina of dogs and owners alike.**

Below, left to right: **Agility trials keep dogs in good condition and teach owners and dogs to work together.** *Bottom:* **Swimming class helps dogs who may be wary of the water to overcome their fears.** *Opposite, top, left to right:* **A motley crew of canine campers take their ease; the camp's Shetland collie contingent gathers for a group photo; dogs and their owners learn the moves for a trans-species macarena.** *Opposite, below:* **Their swimming lesson behind them, two campers watch the action from the sidelines.**

the happiest dog, with the best life," she says. She is a strong advocate of the American Kennel Club's Canine Good Citizen Test, feeling it can be used to certify dogs to allow them into housing and hotels.

Loring once toured the United States and Canada with two timber wolves as an environmental educator. She opened Camp Gone to the Dogs in 1990 as "a place where we can treat dogs to all they deserve, and where humans get to go along for the ride."

"The nice thing about camp," one repeat camper says, "is that you can talk about your dog as much as you like and no one's eyes glaze over."

"Thanks for giving me a place to spend the perfect vacation with my senior citizens, Muffin, Cappie, and Echo," another camper wrote Loring. "Everyone put up with their old-dog quirks. It was a dream come true."

Loring's staff of professional dog trainers, vets, breeders, and animal therapists

At the costume party that wraps up the week at dog camp, spectacular outfits, many made by the dog owners, are the norm. *Below, left to right:* **Dalmatians as dudes; schnauzer as escaped convict; King Charles spaniel as party animal.** *Opposite:* **Chinese shar-pei as an elephant and King Charles spaniels as royals.**

are uniform in their philosophy and approach to the campers. "Fairness to the dogs and love for them in our hearts come before anything else," she says. "We use only positive training methods—treats, toys, play, and petting. Our primary reason for being at camp is to have a good time."

The high rate of returning campers every year—70 percent—suggests that every person and animal has a good time. "Fun is the name of the game," Loring reiterates. "If your dog's tail isn't up, we're doing something wrong."

IN THE DOGHOUSE

The peephole in the door, shaped like a dog biscuit, gives the place away. Log Cabin, one of a handful of cottages where guests can stay at Twin Farms, the award-winning country hotel in Barnard, Vermont, is a fantasy come true for dog lovers.

Inside this "quintessential cabin in the woods," as Twin Farms managing directors Shaun and Beverley Matthews call it, a humorous canine theme subtly asserts itself throughout. Covering the floor of the spacious main room is a plush rug with a pattern of pawprints. Overhead is a chandelier with small metal dog heads mounted on it. At one end of the room, overlooking a sumptuous bed, is a 19th-century tile painting, *Beware of the Dog*, based on a mosaic uncovered in the ruins of the House of the Poet in Pompeii. At the other end, dog figures prance across the mantel of a fireplace, itself furnished with

Above and right: **The Log Cabin at Twin Farms in Vermont makes liberal, and humorous, use of canine iconography throughout. One of eight distinctive cottages at the country inn, it was built from hundred-year-old salvaged lumber from North Carolina.**

andirons in the form of seated wolves. On the sofa near the hearth is a circa 1880 carriage robe with a large, doleful image of a hound.

"Our staff sometimes finds that guests in Log Cabin will turn that robe over during their stay," Beverley reports, explaining, "It's not that they don't like the robe, but the shiny plastic buttons that were sewn into the fabric for the dog's eyes make some guests feel as if the dog is following them around with its gaze as they move about the room."

What makes the canine collection at Twin Farms especially fascinating, from a design point of view, is that it transcends time periods, geographical locations, and aesthetic styles, without becoming a mishmash of discordant notes. Highly valuable works of art by noted artists are juxtaposed with interesting but more commonplace expressions. When a collector achieves this balance, the materials are afforded the same dignity and respect. The flea market entries, in fact, help to keep the serious elements in the collection from coming across as stuffy.

The Log Cabin gives the impression that a single collector with a loving vision of dogs amassed all the things in it over a lifetime. Guests who have stayed here, even those who have never owned a dog of their own, attest to the power of the space to conjure up memories of dogs, both real and imagined. For dog fanciers, there are enough different breeds represented in the collection to satisfy many tastes.

Twin Farms, which opened in 1993, has a history of warm country hospitality dating back to the 1920s, when the original 1795 farmhouse was acquired by Sinclair Lewis, America's first Nobel Prize–winning author, and his wife, the pioneering female journalist Dorothy Thompson. The two threw lavish parties for the literary set of the day, including H. L. Mencken, Rebecca West, and J. Vincent Sheean. Thompson called the place "the best expression in life of both of us—beautiful, comfortable, hospitable, and unpretentious," and, many years later, it measured up to that standard once again, thanks to a multimillion-dollar makeover. In 1974, the property was bought as a vacation home by the Twigg-Smith family of Honolulu, Hawaii, descendants of the missionaries Asa and Lucy Thurston, who first brought Christianity to the islands in 1820. Thurston Twigg-Smith, the current paterfamilias, ran a vast newspaper empire in Honolulu prior to the acquisition. Avid contemporary art and folk art collectors, Twigg-Smith and his wife lent many pieces from their private collections (they own the Contemporary Museum in Honolulu) to decorate Twin Farms. They commissioned architect Alan Wanzenberg and designer Jed Johnson to refurbish the main house and barn and build eight freestanding cottages of wood and stone throughout the 300-acre property. Now there are paintings by Milton Avery, David Hockney, and Roy Lichtenstein on the walls, rugs handmade in Guatemala on the floors, and decorative items from around the world sprinkled through the guest rooms.

Dogs are a recurring theme, not just in Log Cabin but throughout the resort, as in paintings by David Bates, Donald Roller Wilson, William B. Hoyt, and others. Stone dogs and a bronze sculpture, "Huneck's Dog Arthur," by Stephen Huneck, keep the vigil at the back entrance to the main house, with its panoramic view of Mount Ascutney in the distance. A William Wegman photograph of a weimaraner on an exercise bike greets visitors to the resort's fitness center.

Top right: **Maple, a Labrador retriever belonging to the managing directors, is Twin Farms' unofficial greeter.** *Above left:* **Cast-iron dogs parade on the fireplace mantel, along with a familiar foe.** *Above right:* **A metal magazine rack with poodle attributes.**

"We hoped to give guests an experience they wouldn't commonly have in New England," says Wanzenberg. His late partner's eclectic interiors, utterly different for each cottage and suite, accomplish just that by gracefully blending folk art with contemporary art, antiques with custom furniture, lush fabrics, murals, and exquisite woodwork. And probably no single cottage quite so amuses and captivates as Log Cabin.

"Dog lovers do gravitate to that cottage," says Beverley, "and many of them ask if they can bring their own dogs with them when they come to stay. Alas, we do not allow pets on the property, but I do tell them we will provide one for company—Maple, our own yellow Lab—and they usually understand."

The no-pets rule at Twin Farms is easy to understand, given the luxury of the accommodations—who wants a dog tearing up a $35,000 sofa? But, increasingly, there are high-end resorts that welcome canines with open arms, according to *Dog Fancy*. As examples, the magazine cites the Cypress Inn, Carmel Valley, California; the Lorelei Resort, Treasure Island, Florida; the Banner Elk Inn, Banner Elk, North Carolina; and the Four Seasons Hotel, Washington, D.C. The Lorelei has a

Top: **The peephole in the door announces the cottage's whimsical theme.** *Above:* **The Log Cabin's carved chair, chandelier, and several paintings, including a classic scene of a Newfoundland coming to the rescue, all bear the imprint of one dog or another.**
Opposite: **Responsible for all the interiors at Twin Farms, the late designer Jed Johnson was himself a dog lover and had collected many of the objects found in the Log Cabin, including volumes for its bookshelves, such as Thurber's *Dogs* and *The Book of the Poodle*. Even the challenging jigsaw puzzle that comes with the room has a canine motif.**

swimming pool for dogs, grooming services, and an on-site veterinarian. The Cypress Inn, started by the actress and animal lover Doris Day, makes pet sitters available to its guests.

But as dog-friendly as these and other fine resorts may be, none offers accommodations with quite the canine ambience that is found in the doghouse at Twin Farms. The designer's affection for dogs reveals itself in every detail, without however overwhelming a visitor. Log Cabin might well be the last arf on the subject of decorating with dogs.

Twin Farms is an expensive indulgence, as might be expected of a place accorded five-star rating by Mobil year after year, and rated number one in the United States for resort properties by the estimable Zagat. But even without a pooch of their own, few guests who can afford to stay in Log Cabin fail to succumb to the romance of the dog. If it is not the dog pillows that entice them or the busts of dogs mounted on the walls, it is the fireside jigsaw puzzle depicting a variety of dog breeds playing poker and smoking cigars. Or the hound on the sofa, following their every move . . .

PORTRAIT
OF A DOG

Christine Merrill's dogs—Louie, a Pomeranian, and Liebchen, a papillon-spaniel mix—sit underfoot while Charlie, her yellow-naped Amazon parrot, squawks in the background. Christine is putting the finishing touches on a portrait of Bear, a mixed-breed with a lot of foxhound in him, in her Baltimore studio.

Louie and Liebchen have already been immortalized in oil; their portraits hang elsewhere in the house along with other tributes to pets past. Christine painted *Les Chiens des Anges,* showing winged canines ascending to heaven, after she lost Pom Pom, a black Pomeranian she had grown up with, who died at age eighteen. *Homer at Merridell,* which hangs over a mantel, was done in memory of a large bassett hound that had come along a bit later, a departure of

Above: **The artist produces fifteen to twenty commissions a year in her Baltimore studio, working obsessively to capture all the nuances of the dogs so prized by her clients.** *Above right:* **Many of Christine Merrill's early paintings are scattered through her house, including *Les Chiens des Anges,* a picture she made after one of her first dogs, Pom Pom, died at age eighteen.** *Below right:* **American Bred, a portrait done in 1990, features an outline of the United States on the dog's side. Bagpipes on the table date from Christine's youth, when she was an accomplished bagpipe player.**

sorts. "I wasn't used to his make and model," she notes. "Small dogs I can pick up and hug are my normal style. Homer was like a Chevy Suburban compared to a sports coupe."

As for Bear, he had been rescued from an animal shelter in Virginia and was now getting the royal treatment at the behest of his owner, who happened to be a collector of 18th- and 19th-century sporting art. Merrill herself works in a style reminiscent of the English painters of the 18th century and is zealous in her attention to detail and finish.

"I'm trying to get that sweet look in his face, because that's what the owner sees and that's how she's described him to me." Christine remarks, glancing from the canvas to some snapshots she had taken of the dog. Usually she visits clients in their home, taking pictures of the dog and getting a feeling for the emotional bond between owner and pet. "That's why I love to hear all about the dogs—where they came from, where they sleep, how often they're walked, what they eat, what their favorite toys are." Her consultations often provide details that she will include in the background of a painting, such as the likeness of a house where owner and pet live. Merrill produces a preliminary charcoal sketch and sends it to the client for comment. Then she begins painting her subject in oil. "Oil has a permanency that people appreciate the more because the life span of dogs is so much shorter than our own."

Although her portraits fetch from $6,000 to $10,000 or more, Merrill believes that love, not money, motivates the commissions she receives. "Dogs are always there for you," she says. "I try to capture their 'I love you' look that says, 'You're the one for me; there's no other owner but you.'"

Merrill, who has loved drawing and painting ever since she was a child, went on to receive her formal training in classical realism at Baltimore's Schuler School of Fine Arts. She began to specialize in dog portraiture in 1987, after the *New York Times* ran a photo of one of her paintings that showed a Brittany spaniel, a vizsla, and a Dalmatian in front of a country house. "It was a feature in the lifestyle section on the different ways in which homeowners can have their houses captured in art form," she relates. "It wasn't really about dogs at all, but out of it came so many commissions that I realized I might have something here!"

Represented by the prestigious William Secord Gallery in New York, Merrill has since captured the look of unconditional fidelity on the faces of beagles, pugs, chins, poodles, terriers, and a host of other breeds. She has painted for celebrities such as TV host Oprah Winfrey (cocker spaniel), fashion designer Geoffrey Beene (dachshunds), author Barbara Taylor Bradford (bichon frise), and CBS newsman Bob Schieffer (beagle). But dealing with the rich and famous hasn't changed the way Christine paints.

"It doesn't matter who the client is," she says. "I treat each commission as if I were doing it for the Queen of England."

Below: **Christine prepares to take Liebchen and Louie for one of their daily jaunts in the neighborhood.** *Opposite, clockwise from top left:* **Louie and Liebchen, a papillon-spaniel mix, adopted when it came to Christine's back door as a stray; plaster dog head, made in art school in 1984, and photograph of artist's mother as a child; Charlie, the parrot, with sketches of a client's dog from photographs; Louie, a gift from her father, poses in the Mona Lisa photographer's prop that Christine made in art school.**

CHINA SYNDROME

She is known simply as "the Dog Lady" to dealers and collectors who specialize in canine memorabilia, because of her abiding interest in porcelain figures of dogs. But few of them fully realize the extent of her collection, which numbers in the thousands and occupies virtually every space in the suburban Washington, D.C., house that she shares with her mother and a Jack Russell terrier named Brooks.

"I wish I had ten more rooms," she says, "but I'm not moving. Just the idea of packing thousands of fragile figurines is too unnerving for me!"

The Dog Lady still remembers the day it all began, decades ago, during a family trip to Ocean City, Maryland, when she was eight

Above: **A collection that began with a single porcelain dog, a bloodhound, acquired in 1961, when the owner was eight, now numbers in the thousands, and is still growing.**
Right: **Beginning in 1917, bulldogs by Royal Doulton became symbols of England's resolution in the face of looming German aggression. In 1941, as World War II engulfed Europe, a hat and cigar were added to the figure in a tribute to Winston Churchill.**

Below: **Beginning in the 1920s, Dalmatians, French bulldogs, and Boston terriers were made by the German porcelain manufacturer Rosenthal, and are prized collectibles today.** *Opposite, above:* **Brooks, the family Jack Russell.** *Below left:* **The Irish setter and foxhound are from a sporting dog series modeled by Doris Lindner in 1940 for the English china maker Royal Worcester. The series remained in production until 1957.** *Below right:* **Pottery produced by Mortens Studio in Chicago in the 1940s and '50s is grouped by breed type: hounds and terriers, sporting dogs, and working and herding dogs.** *Following pages:* **A custom-built display case in the living room holds the major portion of a collection of porcelain figures of dogs, assembled over a lifetime and organized primarily by manufacturer.**

years old. "Like most children, I wanted a dog when I was growing up," she recalls, "but at first my parents were against the idea. On that vacation I bought a glass bloodhound in a shop, thinking if I couldn't have a real dog, I could at least have a representation. By the time I was a teenager, I had discovered the porcelain lines of Boehm, Royal Doulton, and other manufacturers, and I just kept collecting them. People always knew what to get me for my birthday or at Christmas."

Although her parents eventually did buy her a puppy—a cocker spaniel named Bobo—her collecting interests never waned. "If I'd had a dog in the beginning, I might have gravitated toward just collecting porcelains of that breed," she observes. "But as it was, I became interested in all breeds." With children of her own, she raised miniature silver poodles for some years, then later lived with bulldogs for a while, but she continued to cast her net globally when it came to breeds.

"Actually, I had been collecting for years before I had a clue that anybody else did it," she relates. "I didn't meet another dog collector until the late 1960s. At that time, looking around flea markets and in shops, I might come across no more than one piece a month. However, it would often be a wonderful piece at an affordable price. Nowadays, with books and price guides covering this and almost every field of collectibles, porcelains have come out of the woodwork, and everything is more expensive."

Collecting sensibly in the field today requires being familiar with the individual histories of the dozens of companies, domestic and foreign, that have made a business of porcelains. It helps to know that the Vienna Porcelain Factory, for example,

founded in 1718, stamps its figurines with a beehive mark with the word "Augarten" in a blue underglaze, or that the largest figurines from the California pottery firm Hagen-Renaker were manufactured from 1954 to 1968. The Dog Lady's reference library contains hundreds of books, catalogs, and other resources detailing the output of porcelain makers over the years. But esthetics also play a part in building a good collection.

Now as then, she believes there are four qualities that make a porcelain dog figure valuable: (1) attractive modeling—the figure has to look good; (2) superior medium—the hard-paste porcelain found in all Rosenthal figures, for example, is much better than cheap ceramics or pottery; (3) rarity—some figures were manufactured in very limited quantities; and (4) breed—there is always more demand for figures of the current popular breeds.

The Internet has become a useful resource for collectors of canine materials such as the Dog Lady's figurines. "I have found the Net to be a great way to buy and sell items that I once had to look for over a period of months," she says. Books, collars, canes, trophies, medallions, rugs, and other antique canine collectibles are being offered at numerous Web sites located around the world. Presented in an auction-style format, and often illustrated with detailed photographs of the objects, the sales of dog items are conducted live, with each sale going to the top bidder. Some objects are offered without reserve on them. After a sale is completed, with payment by credit card or check, the item is sent to the buyer, usually with an option to return the object if the terms of the sale were not met.

In addition, the Internet chatrooms dedicated to dog antiques and collectibles offer collectors the chance to become better informed about the fields that interest them, as well as a source for swapping items. Even fine 19th-century dog paintings can be seen, evaluated, and purchased with a simple click of a mouse these days. Not only have dealers in dog collectibles increasingly turned to the Internet to conduct commerce, but some have cut back on their participation in dog shows and antiques shows because they can buy and sell merchandise more efficiently over the Net.

The Dog Lady has a particular weakness for figurines showing dogs at play. "The breeds most often depicted this way are the toy dogs and the terriers," she says. "Their joy at playing with a colorful ball is contagious." Noting that almost every manufacturer has produced at least one dog playing with a ball, she observes, "Balls were often seen during the 1930s Art Deco period, with dogs and other animals sitting atop them." One of the most beautiful of all dog porcelains, she believes, is a Pekingnese with a green ball under its paw, made by Rosenthal.

Although the porcelains are her stock in trade, the Dog Lady hasn't been able to resist adding dog statues, drawings, paintings, and other objects to her collection.

Below, left to right: **A collection of medallions given as prizes at dog shows around the world;** *Laying Down the Law,* **a 19th-century print by Sir Edwin Landseer, with a poodle in the role of judge, and a bronze sculpture of an Italian greyhound from 1860; in the kitchen, early English Cauldon plates, an array of bronzes from the 1930s, and various old collars, including one associated with Saint Bernards.** *Opposite:* **Augmenting the owner's porcelain collection are other objects of canine beauty, including a pair of bulldogs, enamel on silver, created by George Wright in the early 1900s.**

She does draw the line at some things, however. "I remember seeing a stuffed Great Dane for sale for $750 at an antiques shop," she reports. "It had been the mascot for some hotel in Philadelphia and now was posturing upon a massive tilted base. But I liked the handsome metal collar around its neck, so I told the dealer, 'I don't think I could live with the dog, but I'd love to have the collar.' Well, at first he wouldn't separate the things, but many months later I discovered he had gotten rid of the Great Dane at auction and kept the collar." She added another treasure to her collection.

PART TWO

Dogs
on the
TOWN

●◆●

In the popular Thin Man movies of the 1930s and 1940s, William Powell and Myrna Loy played a suave amateur sleuth and his breezy, socially well-connected wife, living and drinking martinis in Manhattan, but their image as the ultimate urbane couple would not have been complete without Asta, their wire-haired fox terrier. Just as Dorothy's cairn terrier in *The Wizard of Oz*, Toto, represents the perfect country dog in popular culture, Asta is the ultimate city dog, an elegant purebred with attitude.

Below: **In its trophies and paintings (this one, by Maud Earl, of a standard poodle who won Best in Show at the Westminster Dog Show in 1935), the American Kennel Club exemplifies the elegance of the purebred dog.** *Opposite, above and below:* **Grooming salons like Le Chien in New York and boutiques like Angel Dog in Boston cater to the growing population of city dwellers who own dogs and want them to look their best.**

Nick Charles, Powell's character, actually walked Asta himself, taking the dog for long strolls in Central Park, a hiatus from home life that also gave him the chance to call his bookie to bet on the ponies. If those movies were remade in the canine culture of today's big cities, it would probably be more believable for a professional dog walker to handle Asta. In fact, the infrastructure of canine goods and services in cities like New York is so vast and sophisticated that a dog like Asta could go weeks without seeing its owners and still have a great time.

Animal behaviorist Desmond Morris believes that dogs first became the welcome companions of city dwellers in the aftermath of the Industrial Revolution, providing 19th-century urbanites with a nostalgic reminder of country life.

"Walking the dog in the park became almost the last remnant of rural pleasures left for those trapped in the city whirl," he has observed. "In an environment paved with stone and walled with bricks and mortar, the need for some sort of contact with the natural world was a powerful one, and dogs went a long way to fulfilling this need."

But when motor vehicles replaced horses and carriages in the 20th century, the pace of city life quickened. Dogs came to be seen as an inconvenient extravagance.

"Why on earth would you want a dog in the city?" was once the gauntlet thrown down to any city dweller who might have expressed interest in getting a dog. Think of the dedication it takes, first of all. Walking a dog at least twice a day in all kinds of weather and picking up after it are no problem for suburban or rural dog owners.

City life is loud with sirens and squealing tires, short on grass, and long on hazards and inconveniences for dogs as well as for their owners. Crowded sidewalks are molten in summer, covered with ice and harmful salt in winter. Steps of marble and granite can be slippery and forbidding. Elevators in apartment buildings have a jolting, claustrophobic menace about them. And waiting around every corner, to further distract and intimidate the hapless city dog, are legions of hissing cats, aggressive pigeons, and mean kids.

But times have changed again. Dogs have become fully vested members of the urban community. Many are companions for a rising number of childless adults who live and work in cities, as singles or couples. Cities are more tolerant of dogs, by law, than they have ever been. In some places, legal rulings have paved the way for people to have dogs in apartments that were previously off limits to pets. A handful of smaller

Above: **The nearly ubiquitous presence of dogs in America's major cities has spawned a large and complex infrastructure of canine services and suppliers.** *Opposite:* **Professional dog walkers have become a common sight in the parks of New York and other cities.**

companies based in cities even allow employees to bring dogs with them to work.

The unique society formed by contemporary urban dogs was captured from a dog's point of view in the novel *Real Estate* by Jane DeLynn. After the beleaguered administration of the city described in the novel decides to crack down on unruly dogs in its park system by strictly enforcing its leash laws, a dog named Jack finds that life has changed for the worse:

One day, just like that, the unspeakable had occurred. . . . He looked around; other dogs were on their leashes too. Great sadness there was in the park that day. Jack was still brought near and allowed to sniff other dogs, but the rituals of teeth-baring and attacking were almost instantly cut short; there was no running or demonstrating of hunting skills; worst of all, there was none of that camaraderie of dogs being together as dogs, away and separate from humans.

In truth, most city dogs spend most of their time with their human friends and family, but they are not entirely denied the pleasures of running with the pack. Although every major city has laws requiring owners to keep their dogs on a lead in public places, many parks have established fenced dog runs where unleashed dogs can freely jolly it up with other dogs. In parks blessed with large open areas, authorities often look the other way if dogs are not bothering other park users, as is usually the case very early in the morning or late at night. Prospect Park in Brooklyn, for example, turns into a vast canine playground at the crack of dawn.

"They come in a zillion shapes and sizes," says one lifelong Brooklyn dweller of

the dogs that show up at a nearby park early every morning for an hour of unfettered socializing and play. "What's remarkable is that they all get along," she adds. "In summer, when people bring food into the park for picnics or cookouts, some dogs get into squabbles over chicken bones and other scraps, but most of the fights are settled peacefully by the owners. Most of the dogs really seem to want to get along. People who bring them to the park all the time know each other, not by their own names, but by the names of their dogs."

Paris was perhaps the first city to open its heart, along with its cafés and bistros, to dogs, but New York surely has surpassed the French capital in its enthusiasm for the species, with an estimated one million dogs now residing in households in the five boroughs. But the ubiquitous canine presence in New York also reflects a national trend; the No Dogs Allowed signs are coming down in cities all across the country.

Dogs are an integral part of the urban social scene. People don't just walk their dogs; they escort them, taking their canine chums on shopping trips and showing up with them at dinner parties. Indeed, dogs have become the real party animals. Events to raise money for homeless or abandoned animals, like the ASPCA's annual walkathon in Central Park, billed as "Woofstock," draw people and their dogs by the thousands. Animal Wingding, a street fair in San Francisco's Mission District to benefit the local SPCA, attracts more than 40,000 people, along with their dogs, cats, and assorted other pets. The day of food, music and fun includes a singing-dog contest and canine Frisbee-catching demonstrations. Reflecting the way many city people feel about dogs in general these days, one fairgoer reports, "It is a howl."

LIBRARY WITH PEDIGREE

Before its recent move to new headquarters, the library of the American Kennel Club, perched on the tenth floor of the New York Life building in Manhattan, enjoyed a commanding view of the Empire State Building, but few visitors bothered to look out the windows. With more than 16,000 items of canine life and lore on shelves, in cabinets, hanging on the walls, and otherwise on exhibit, the collection contains so much fascinating material, at least for dog lovers, that no one had a chance to appreciate the view.

"This library is made up of a lot of things besides books," notes library administrator Barbara Kolk. "We're lucky so many people donated things that we would never have been able to buy."

Such gems range from two imposing silver trophies commissioned by the Bulldog Club of America in 1890, complete with detailed

Above: **Champion Joe II, an 1899 painting by Lucy Waller of a standard poodle with corded coat, is one of many works of art in the AKC library.** *Right:* **The extensive collection of dog books includes many titles that are works of art in themselves.**

Above left: **Old books about fictional dogs celebrate the heroic traits authors have found in virtually every canine breed.** *Above:* **Pop-up and fold-out features were enticing innovations in early dog books such as *Cassell's New Book of the Dog*, "a comprehensive natural history of British dogs and their foreign relatives," and *The Complete Dog Fancier's Companion*, published in 1819.** *Left:* **A stud book from 1878 lists more than 1,400 registered dogs.** *Opposite, above:* **Maud Earl's painting *Silent Sorrow* depicts King Edward's favorite terrier following the monarch's death in 1910.** *Below:* **The skeleton of Belgrave Joe, the patriarch of the modern fox terrier breed, who lived from 1869 to 1888.**

carvings of the breed in pugnacious guard dog mode, to the skeleton of Belgrave Joe, the dog considered the patriarch of the modern fox terrier breed. Joe died in England in 1888 after nearly twenty productive years as a stud. The skeleton was used as a teaching tool at the Royal Veterinary College in England before finding its way to America.

Handsome dog paintings also grace the library. One, an oil portrait of a terrier, was executed by the well-known English artist Maud Earl shortly after the death of King Edward VII in 1910. *Silent Sorrow* depicts the king's favorite dog, Caesar, seated with his head in mournful repose upon the cushion of a chair.

More recent donations include trophies, memorabilia, and official documents of the United States Lakeland Terrier Club, dating from the 1930s, and photos, news clippings, and stud cards of prominent Irish setters of times past. Both passels of material came from daughters of men who were deeply involved with dogs.

"Some member clubs send yearbooks and other material on their breeds," Barbara says, "which become valuable archives for the AKC as well as for the individual clubs many years down the road."

Founded in 1884, the AKC is a "club of clubs," with some 500 member clubs and more than 4,000 affiliated clubs. The organization sanctions more than 13,000 dog events annually, ranging from conformation dog shows to performance events such as field trials for sporting breeds, herding trials for herding breeds, and earth dog tests for small terriers and dachshunds. It maintains a huge purebred dog registry—the largest in the world—to keep track of the bloodlines of the more than 140 breeds recognized by the club.

PUTTING ON THE DOG

It could be called the dawn of the Reign of Terrier. Early Sunday morning on a crisp fall day in Ambler, Pennsylvania, the all-terrier show of the Montgomery County Kennel Club is about to begin on the campus of Temple University.

Parking lots on the campus are jammed with jumbo trailers and vans, their license plates telling of treks from near and far. People stream out of the parking lots with terriers of all makes and models in their arms, on lead, or in tow inside wheeled kennels. There are the familiar Scotties and schnauzers, the lamblike Bedlington terriers, the chesty, pirate-faced bull terriers, silky-haired Skyes, tiny, spunky Westies and cairns, Norwich terriers (ears up), Norfolk terriers (ears down), and many others. In all, twenty-six different terrier breeds will compete in the seventeen rings set up on the showgrounds.

Above and right: **One of the oldest and most prestigious purebred shows of the year is Montgomery County Kennel Club's all-terrier show, with as many as twenty-six terrier breeds on parade, including Bedlington terriers, noted for their curly, woolly coat.**

Below, from far left to right: **During the all-terrier show, parking lots on the suburban campus of Temple University, where the show is staged, are filled with cars, vans, and trailers declaring their breed loyalty to the world.** *Bottom left:* **Soft-coated wheaten terriers start out in life with black, straight coats that gradually turn wavy and wheaten—the shade of wheat ripening in a sunny field.**
Bottom right: **Airedale terriers strut their stuff in the show ring under the watchful eye of an omnipotent judge.**

Few weekends go by without several large, exuberant packs of dog owners, breeders, trainers, handlers, stewards, and judges getting together somewhere. The American Kennel Club alone each year sanctions more than 11,000 events, which draw nearly 2 million entries annually. The most prestigious fixture of all is the Westminster Kennel Club dog show in New York City, a sparkling affair held each February at Madison Square Garden. But when it comes to outdoor events, the Montgomery County terrier show is one of the best for conveying the drama and spectacle of the purebred sport.

Early in the morning, long lines form at the concessions for hot coffee and pastries. Old friends stop to exchange greetings while their dogs stand off warily from each other. Dog show officials rush in with flowers, signs, and trophies to embellish the prize tables inside the colorful tents, each table fastidiously maintained by a different breed club. At a discreet remove, merchants set up shop to hawk terrier jewelry, terrier sculptures, terrier paintings, terrier books, terrier hats, and terrier T-shirts.

Another long line develops in front of the tent of the governing kennel club, where exhibitors and visitors purchase copies of the indispensable bible, a 720-page show catalog with a soft red vinyl cover bearing the MCKC's raised silver seal and a handsome profile of the show's first Best in Show winner back in 1929, a wire fox terrier named Iveshead Scamp. As the competition unfolds, showgoers sit with their copies of the show catalog open on their laps, some of them making frequent and minute notations on its pages.

Throughout the day, beginning with the first class of soft-coated wheaten terriers in ring 1 at 8:00 A.M., the action never stops. With various breeds and classes being judged simultaneously, it is impossible to observe every activity, and no one really tries. Most showgoers stick with their biases, watching the breeds they own or admire, or just settling in to observe a particular judge assess each class and each dog in the class in a methodical, inscrutable, yet utterly convincing manner.

At dog shows, judges evaluate a dog's conformation—or how closely its physical structure conforms to its breed standard. The standard is a detailed description of a breed, written by the breed's parent club, which takes into account general appearance, coat, color, gait, temperament, and a host of other factors. This day, whenever a judge makes a decision, often with a mere twitch of the hand or nod of the head, there are bursts of applause, gasps of delight and disappointment, hallelujahs and sighs, smiles and regrets—and no means for appealing the verdict.

While the action unfolds in the show rings, handlers and owners groom other dogs in several tents. Portable generators power the hair dryers. Some dog owners present their own dogs in the ring at shows, but many hire professional handlers, who make the job look as easy as walking the pooch after breakfast.

By early afternoon the weather is positively summery. Over at ring 16, Bob and Dolores Hope are seated in the sun, awaiting the appearance of their daughter, who is showing Norwich terriers. Perhaps because of the heat, the well-known comedian—in his nineties, after all—dozes off from time to time, but he comes to attention when the judging commences. And afterward, when his daughter places her dog in his lap, he positively beams, and as he pets her dog, one of America's most beloved entertainers is youthful again.

Opposite, above and below:
At most major dog shows, professional groomers are enlisted to prepare the entrants for the ring; the advent of lightweight portable generators has made it possible for dogs to be shampooed, blow-dried, brushed, and combed immediately prior to showtime.

PICTURE THIS

Valerie Shaff did not set out in life to be a photographer of dogs, but her genius for capturing on film the individual character of canines has made her sepia portraits highly coveted works of art, as well as mementos that owners cherish.

"Oh, my God, that's exactly what Pogo—or Scamp or Henry or Lucky—is all about!" the typical owner exclaims upon seeing the finished image of a dog that Valerie has wrought with her Hasselblad, her lighting, and her sure instincts for plumbing the four-legged soul.

"I work to establish a good rapport with the dog," she explains, "so that the portrait session is enjoyable for both of us. Once that happens, it is easier to bring out a dog's true character, whether it is in a shy or skeptical gaze or some other authentic expression."

Growing up in Hastings-on-Hudson, New York, Shaff remembers

Above and right: **Dog portraitist Valerie Shaff set up shop in a show window at Barneys in New York to photograph dozens of dogs belonging to the department store's preferred customers. The antic experience over two consecutive weekends was captured on video by a friend and eventually became a short entered in the Nantucket Film Festival.**

Taffy, a golden retriever, as "a very important member of the family, from about the time I was five to fifteen." She went to Bard College to study painting, but ended up graduating with a degree in photography. Living in rural Greene County in upstate New York after college, she became fascinated by "all the small-time barnyards in that part of the country, each with a little bit of everything." She felt somewhat isolated and lonely, she recalls, but training her camera on farm animals helped to dispel the blues. "I made these very innocent medium-format portraits of the animals, and people just went crazy for the prints."

At about the same time, a friend with a liver-spotted Dalmatian named Coco asked Valerie to photograph the dog. "Just for fun, I decided to take some action shots of Coco going over jumps," she relates. "But when I made prints, I was amazed at how heroic an image I had created."

One thing led to another. In 1995, friends of hers who owned George, then a mail-order store specializing in products with a dog theme, decided to open a retail outlet in San Francisco. Valerie recounts, "We set up a photo booth of sorts for the opening and invited people to bring in their dogs for portaits."

Since then Shaff has conducted daylong portrait sessions for dogs at Barneys, in both New York and Los Angeles, acquired an agent and a gallery (Bridgewater Lustberg Gallery in Manhattan), and has published her first book of dog portraits, entitled *If Only You Knew How Much I Smell You.*

"It's fun to be doing something that I didn't initiate with commercial intentions," she declares. "I started making the portraits and it just took off."

Below: **Marcel, a French bulldog with a relaxed disposition, proved to be an easy subject for the photographer to work with. Above the staging area is a portrait of a bull terrier named Louise, shot "dead on," says Shaff, "because Louise is a very straightforward and unintimidated character."** *Opposite, above:* **Silhouettes of thirteen friends and a mutt named Kitty share space with photographs of dogs and friends in Shaff's studio. The cutouts were made by a silhouette artist at a Christmas party the photographer threw to thank the women "who got me through a difficult year."** *Below left:* **The portrait of Kitty with her owner was taken in a stream behind a country house Shaff once lived in.** *Below right:* **Between exhibitions, dog portraits are stored temporarily in a convenient hallway.**

URBAN
LAIR

Show dogs and pets are memorialized in art throughout the gracious five-story brownstone of The Leash, a club for sportsmen and dog fanciers. Canine trophies and bronzes add character to mantels and tables. The library is stocked with old books on dogs and other sporting subjects. Over the bar is a portrait of eleven wire-haired fox terriers, the champion dogs of an early member.

Founded in 1925, at the peak of Prohibition, the club originally arranged for members to keep their liquor in individual wooden lockers tagged with brass nameplates of favorite dogs. "Or favorite horses, yachts, kennels—anything but the member's actual name," relates a current member of the club. "Later, when the club moved its headquarters to the brownstone, the doors were removed from the lockers and used as paneling for the bar room in the new location."

Above: **A dog club's liquor lockers from Prohibition days, no longer in use, still bear the names of bygone dogs.** *Right:* **A portrait by F. C. Fuirmang of the bulldog Champion L'Ambassadeur hangs in the club dining room.** *Following pages:* **In a library devoted to books on dogs, hunting, and fishing, a painting of an English setter by the early-20th-century American artist Percival Rosseau takes center stage.**

Having a comfortable place to take a nip, unmolested by the police and the other forces for teetotaling in that era, was in fact one of the lesser purposes of the new club. The founders were serious dog men—breeders and exhibitors—unhappy with what they considered the very shaky management practices of the American Kennel Club at the time. Their original idea was to put pressure on the AKC to resolve a host of problems that were occurring in the rapidly expanding sport of purebreds, including uneven and incompetent judging at shows, difficulties with shows and schedules, wasteful fiscal policies, and many other bones of contention.

Letters to the AKC *Gazette* at the time underlined some of the controversies in the AKC as it sought to keep up with and control the ever-expanding world of pure-bred dogs. Some accused the license committee, which supervised the temporary and permanent granting of licenses to judges, of being inaccessible and unaccountable. Others debated the lack of independent voting by delegates, the pros and cons of muzzling dogs, the question of whether or not to crop ears and tails, methods of treating distemper, and the ballooning size of dog shows.

The club's incorporation documents did not mention the AKC by name but did state its goals forthrightly: "to promote interest in the thoroughbred dog; to study and apply principles of scientific breeding; to consider the various problems of the breeder and fancier; and to forward and support all which makes for the highest interest, standards, and conduct of the sport of breeding, working, racing, and showing dogs."

Opposite and below: **In the bar, paintings of an early member's pointers and setters grace one wall, by German-American artist Edmund H. Osthaus. The group painting of fox terriers over the bar, though undated and unsigned, is a reminder that the three founding members of the club were important breeders and exhibitors of this breed. Directly beneath it, *Gamester,* painted in 1880, is annotated, "Winner First Prize Westminster Kennel Club 1878 and Special Prize Westminster Kennel Club 1879."**

IMPORT & DOMESTIC BEER

BASS (U.K.)
BECKS (GER.)
CARLSBURG ELEPHANT (DAN.)
FOSTERS (AUST.)
GUINNESS STOUT (IRE.)
HEINEKENS (HOLL.)
KIRIN (JAPAN)
MICHELOB (U.S.)
PILSNER URQUELL (CHEC.)

The fifteen founding members of The Leash had firsthand experience of the AKC's problems. Three of the men were AKC directors and six were AKC delegates. Several others were dog show judges. There were breeders of various terriers as well as a Doberman breeder and an English cocker breeder. All of them were active dog show participants. Within a year, there were more than a hundred members, most of whom were also active in various phases of showing and breeding dogs. Many had large kennels and owned successful Best in Show winners.

In the same period, however, the AKC moved to address the problems that its critics had brought to light. AKC president John E. DeMund admitted to mistakes "in the conducting of kennel affairs" and expressed the hope that "there will be even more of a Christ-like spirit throughout the world of dogs." Accepting this olive branch, the club established as a working alternative to the AKC dropped its role as watchdog and agitator for change.

"At that time, the character of the club took form as an institution of convivial sportsmen," an early member related, "who promptly forgot the original idea of political pressure on the American Kennel Club and just naturally gathered together for fun."

When members were not content to sit in the bar, studying the old brass plates, or in the soft leather library chairs, perusing biographies of Henry Cabot Lodge or Theodore Roosevelt, they were off on fishing trips for trout in Pennsylvania or the Catskills, or for tarpon and bonefish in the Florida Keys, or on shooting expeditions for pheasant, duck, and quail.

"The club founded on discord and conflict," wrote Sari B. Tietjen in the AKC *Gazette*, years later, "was able to advance onward and upward to become what it is today—a comfortable, relaxed club comprised of like-minded gentlemen who know how to enjoy their clubhouse, sporting, and social activities—and animals."

The Leash sponsored its own dog show from 1930 to 1964, holding the event every year on the grounds of some member's estate. The show was as much a social outing as a competition, and was revived as a biennial affair in 1971, with the help of the Westminster Kennel Club as co-sponsor. The Leash also presents a perpetual sterling silver challenge cup of Georgian design to the American-bred dog or bitch winning Best in Show at Westminster.

On the lighter side, Sari Tietjen, herself an experienced dog show judge, reported that at one joint show, a Westminster Best in Show winner was declared in a special pet dog class that followed its own rules of conformation. She explained, "This is the class where winning is predicated on having the cutest face, softest fur, longest tail, and/or sweetest child on the other end of the lead."

Below: **The Trapp Cup and the Philadelphia Gun Club Presidents Cup add their shine to a piano laden with old standards.** *The Hunter's Return,* **painted in 1971, depicts a club member returning from the field with his dogs, Briar, Sam, and Corn.** *Opposite:* **A 1953 painting of Airedale terriers overlooks the bar entrance. The largest trophy on the side table is the Vanderbilt Hotel Cup, won by Mrs. Tyler Morse and her sheepdog in 1912 in a show sponsored by the Ladies Kennel Association of America.**

WALKING THE DOG

While attending the Westminster Kennel Club dog show in the early 1970s, Shirlee and Larry Kalstone ran into an acquaintance sporting a distinguished-looking walking stick with the carved-wood likeness of a whippet's head on it.

The Kalstones, who were breeding and showing whippets and poodles at the time, paused to chat with their friend. Walter Reznikoff had worked for Abercrombie & Fitch in the glory days of that sporting emporium, when products and accoutrements for dogs were an important part of the store's inventory. ("Dogs' Day is every day in our store," an early catalog once proclaimed.) He now showed dogs and was so esteemed for his knowledge that the Duke and Duchess of Windsor often left their pugs in his care when they traveled.

Above: **Made by Fabergé, a 19th-century heavy silver bulldog with ruby eyes bears the mark of Julius A. Rappoport, head silversmith, who fabricated many of the Fabergé large silver animal pieces. When the dog's lower jaw is exposed, its tongue extends and reveals an anatomically correct mouth.**
Opposite: **A spectacular collection of canine walking sticks includes two greyhounds, one a rare silver piece made in 1900 and signed Tiffany & Co., the other of silver and ivory from about the same period, and, below them, a finely detailed Brussels griffon head in silver from about 1890.**

Above: The finest hundred or so canes of the Kalstone collection are displayed in the three tiers of an umbrella stand originally belonging to an Edwardian men's club in Piccadilly, London. Above it, in a turn-of-the-century gouache by Fanny Moody entitled *Playmates,* a standard poodle in old show trim seeks to keep possession of the walking stick it is playing with. The portrait of English foxhounds, *The Father of the Pack,* is an early hand-colored engraving, circa 1850, after a painting by the well-known 19th-century sporting artist William Barraud.

Above right: **Silk crocheted ribbon parasols, including one with a mother-of-pearl poodle jumping through a gold hoop, and an ivory walking stick with three carved heads of dogs.**

*Right: **The Gatekeeper's Cottage,** a signed painting by George Horlor in 1872, is above **Hamlet,** an exceptionally sensitive oil on canvas, circa 1870, by George Earl, one of the most widely known painters of the day.*

Clockwise from top left: **A system cane with a spirit level in the cross arm for measuring dogs, made for Colonel North, one of the most prominent greyhound breeders and judges in England at the end of the 19th century, and owner of Fullerton, a four-time Waterloo Stakes champion; heads carved in ivory and wood, including a museum-quality bloodhound, carved circa 1875, "one of the two or three most beautifully carved in our collection," says Larry Kalstone; an Irish setter of wood whose tongue waggles when the stick is moved; ornately carved ivory canes showing dogs in action, including a 20th-century German one with an ivory ball handle carved with fifty breeds.**

Chatting with Reznikoff, but unable to take his eyes off the cane, and knowing that the man sold dog antiques on the side, Larry Kalstone finally ventured to ask if it was for sale.

The deal was closed for $65, and shortly after that, an even more impressive, and pricier, cane came their way; this one boasted a beautifully carved pointer head of ivory. Suddenly the Kalstones were on their way to assembling what one expert in the field has called "a jewel of a collection" of canine walking sticks.

"The collection started casually," Shirlee Kalstone observes. "Canes were hard to find in this country, but as it happened, we began traveling to England frequently in connection with Larry's business." At the time he headed Ring 5, a company that manufactured grooming products for pets, and he was setting up distribution for those products abroad. "We discovered shops and dealers specializing in canes in London and, later, Paris," she relates. "We came home with one or two canes from our first trips, and then pretty soon we were bringing back eight or ten at a time."

Today the canes number in the hundreds, the most venerable being a Wilkinson sword cane from the 1700s. Most of the others are tributes to dogs, with some cats thrown in for variety. "We have tried to find canes that depict a true representation of breeds as they existed at the time the canes were made," Shirlee explains. "If the carvings are overly stylized, or exaggerate some of the breed's features, they won't fit in our collection."

Shirlee comes by her knowledge of breed characteristics through professional experience with dogs that began when she was a teenager. "I wanted a miniature poodle," she recalls, "but my parents, who had always had dogs, knew that poodles were expensive to maintain. Although divorced, they agreed that, 'If you want poodles, you'll have to learn to groom them yourself.'"

One summer, during a school vacation, Shirlee talked her way into a position at a dog grooming shop called Poodletown at the corner of Park Avenue and 80th Street in Manhattan. "I started by doing the most menial tasks, such as bathing the dogs, but one day the owner, Joan Saunders Kruger, relented and let me start grooming them, saying I had an eye for dogs." Soon she was grooming Poodletown's premier clients, among them the poodles of Grace Kelly and Elizabeth Taylor.

Shirlee became so proficient at grooming that eventually she opened her own grooming school in her hometown of Pittsburgh. A few years later, after meeting Larry (at a dog show) and marrying, she capitalized on her experience by organizing seminars on the art of grooming dogs. From her first seminar in 1981, Shirlee's Intergroom has grown into an educational conference and trade show that attracts 2,000 participants annually.

Although the dog figures on their walking sticks require no grooming, the Kalstones do handle the collection with tender loving care. Displayed in their city apartment against a background of old dog paintings and other objects with a canine theme, they are a tribute to the centuries-old craftsmanship of their makers and the eternal charm of their breeds. Larry's favorite is a Fabergé bulldog with a tongue that moves. Shirlee's favorite is an ivory . . . cat.

At an auction devoted primarily to dinosaur relics, Larry Kalstone obtained this 35-million-year-old fossil of a dog, authenticated by the Phillips auction house. Calling home, he told Shirlee, who had been wanting a dog, "I just bought one for you."

CITY SIDEWALKS

Living with a dog in a city has never been easier or more agreeable. For one thing, there are so many *other* dog owners in the same boat. A trip to the nearest park, dog run, or sidewalk café is bound to bring one's own dog in contact with the dogs of a dozen other breeds. "Walking my dog is my daily ritual, like reading the morning paper," says one urban dweller, not unconscious of the civic entitlement she has gained from being part of a large canine collectivity, lacking only a secret handshake. They are not mentioned in the U.S. Constitution, but city dogs seem to have entered the ranks of the citizenry, with a full range of rights and hardly any responsibilities.

But the main reason that owning a city dog has become manageable is the proliferation of dog-related services and suppliers in the major cities. Keeping pace with the enhanced status of the urban pooch, canine businesses of all kinds have been established: professional dog

Above and right: **More than ever before, dogs are part of America's urban landscape, as indispensable to daily life in our major cities, seemingly, as the morning newspaper or the afternoon coffee break.**

In New York City, where an estimated one million dogs are kept as pets, a vast dog-care infrastructure is in place, ranging from boutiques and salons to veterinary and day-care services. Canine Styles on Lexington Avenue is one of the oldest city shops to specialize in dog grooming and accessories; it opened for business in 1959.

walkers with Ph.D.'s in animal behavior, gourmet dog food shops, high-fashion grooming salons, full-fledged day-care centers, and animal psychologists—and animal psychics—willing to make house calls. Los Angeles dog owners can drop their dog off at the Dog House for a complete makeover, including massage, manicure, pedicure, and herbal wrap and bath, or at the Total Dog, the city's first canine fitness center, for a soak in a whirlpool and therapy for arthritis, among many other choices. Costs of these services for dogs are hardly negligible. An estimated 10 percent of dog owners in New York City alone spend more than $10,000 a year pampering their pets.

Lisa Gilford opened Le Chien in 1972 primarily as a salon, and stretch limos still pull up to her place daily to deliver dogs for brushouts and manicures, but it has also grown into a fancy goods emporium. Gilford designs and makes dog coats in camel hair and cashmere and creates dog sweaters from Ralph Lauren yarns. She

also has created a full line of dog accessories, from Chanel-inspired leashes to double-strand pearl necklaces, and even has launched a line of dog fragrances, sold exclusively in the shop—Martine for her, Christophe for him.

Angel Dog in Boston is an intimate walk-down shop filled with charm and merchandise imprinted with the likenesses of myriad breeds. There are hand-painted ceramic dinner plates, needlepoint pillows, hand-carved clocks, weather vanes, letter openers, pictures, sculptures, "charm bracelet" dog collars, suspenders, and neckties—and that's just the tip of the iceberg.

"Dogs and people can let down their hair in here," notes Cynthia DesBrisay, who with her husband, Christopher, opened the shop in 1994, "but dogs have the right of way." That is the case anyway with Mr. Crumpet, a golden retriever who can usually be found sunning himself in the canine topiary garden behind the shop, under the protective gaze of an enormous poodle made of ivy and chicken wire.

With outdoor seating and a distinctly canine decor, Manhattan eateries like the Barking Dog Luncheonette on Third Avenue cater to dog owners, even though public health laws forbid bringing pets inside restaurants. In Central Park, the bronze tribute to Balto, a sled dog credited with heroism during a deadly outbreak of diphtheria in Alaska in 1925, always gives pause to people walking their own dogs.

This page and opposite: **In an age preoccupied with health and fitness, dogs and humans help each other to stretch legs and exercise the heart—or just to take the sun. The problem of unwanted or stray dogs in cities is tackled humanely by nonprofit charitable organizations like Bide-A-Wee Home Association, which has operated no-kill animal shelters since 1903.**

"Angel Dog is the first store to devote itself entirely to canine products," states Cynthia, but she notes that it began as much for sentiment as commerce. "Angel Dog is in memory of the five goldens who lived with us for years," she adds. "Winston, M&M, Dimka, Kitty-O, and Sundance went everywhere with us, like Elsa trailing her mistress in *Born Free*. We even took them to the White House for an art reception one year. They were like kids to us, and when we lost them—three of the dogs within eight months of each other—it was devastating."

Aware that the incidence of cancer among dogs is high, the couple decided to sponsor an annual fund-raiser for the benefit of the Harrington Oncologic Center at Tufts University School of Veterinary Medicine. For one such event, they created a large Baltimore appliqué quilt with a heart-shaped opening in the center. For a contribution to Tufts, dog owners had pictures snapped by Cynthia of their pets gazing through the heart.

That same playful optimism pervades the shop. To celebrate Mr. Crumpet's third birthday, the DesBrisays invited the dogs of about a dozen friends over, hired a mariachi band, and passed around grilled steak tips on a silver platter. Dessert was a modified wedding cake topped by a sculptured golden retriever wearing a sombrero.

"And the dogs yipped in all the right places during the songs," Cynthia says.

This page and opposite: **Angel Dog**, on fashionable Charles Street in Boston, was opened by artists Cynthia and Christopher DesBrisay in memory of five golden retrievers who lived with them for years. The owners claim the boutique was the first in the world to devote itself entirely to canine products, and they get no argument about that from their current golden, Mr. Crumpet.

This page and opposite: **Le Chien, on the ground floor of the Trump Plaza, is the dog groomer of choice for canine high society on Manhattan's Upper East Side. The boutique also carries a perfume line created by its owner, Lisa Gilford. The likes of Elizabeth Taylor regularly scents her Maltese with the flowery fragrance named Martine for a poodle Gilford once held dear.**

EAST SIDE GALLERY

"Most people still want a dog portrait that looks like their own dog," says William Secord, the owner of a gallery in New York specializing in 19th-century dog art that champions a realistic presentation of the animal. The English artists George Stubbs and Sir Edwin Landseer were masters of this anatomically correct genre of the period, and today's most successful dog portraitists carry on in a similar style. "Highly stylized or abstract treatments of dogs just don't do it for dog owners. Folk art dogs, for instance, are more likely to appeal to folk art people than to dog people."

Secord's gallery is a magnet for dog people year-round, but it is especially busy during the Westminster Kennel Club dog show every February. Live dogs are welcome here, although Bill adds, "I would

Above: **William Secord, a 1915 portrait of a bulldog by Lilian Cheviot looking over his shoulder, operates the only gallery in the United States devoted exclusively to canine art.** *Above right:* **Paintings from the 19th and early 20th centuries are hung in the floor-to-ceiling Victorian style of the Royal Academy. The pugs, Ms. Tuppence and Ms. Ruby, belong to one of Bill's assistants, Jo-Ann Brown.** *Below right:* **In the front gallery is an oil of Irish and English setters in the field, by Arthur Fitzwilliam Tait, and, over the mantel,** *Henrietta Ham,* **painted circa 1920 by Arthur Wardle.**

prefer if they are well behaved." In addition to the works of the Old Masters of canine painting, the gallery also shows contemporary artists. Secord also represents a select number of contemporary dog portraitists, most notably Barrie Barnett, Christine Merrill, and Joseph H. Sulkowski.

His book, *Dog Painting Art,* identifies three major categories of dog painting. Beginning in the 18th century, hound and sporting dog paintings were commissioned to depict dogs performing at their best, whether foxhounds running after their prey or sporting dogs—setters, spaniels, retrievers, and pointers—working in the field to find birds. During the 19th century, with the rise of dog shows and purebreds, a new type of portrait appeared, one meant to depict the characteristics of individual breeds in general and the finer points of one animal in particular. And finally, aided in no small measure by the patronage of Queen Victoria, an avid dog lover, and other royals, the category of pet portraiture came into being, a style that appealed particularly to England's newly prospering middle class.

"The pet dog might also be purebred," Secord explains, "but in the pet portrait the intention was to depict the dog more casually in a domestic environment." Typically, the pet was shown engaged in routine activities such as sleeping, resting, begging, or performing tricks.

Dog paintings in the United States emerged in similar genres only at later dates, from the sporting dogs of Arthur Fitzwilliam Tait in the latter part of the 19th century to the purebreds of Gustav Muss-Arnholt, Edmund Osthaus, Percival Rosseau, and Edwin Megargee in the early decades of the 20th century.

Opposite: **In the cabinet, Wedgwood plates from the 1940s feature dogs based on the etchings of Marguerite Kirmse, an English-born artist who lived and worked in the United States.** *Below:* **Stick and scarf pins were worn to show off the owners' love for their dogs, such as the Westie signed by W. Essex, the Italian micromosaic of a pug on the large oval pin, and the spaniel of gold, enamel, and diamonds, all made from about 1860 to 1870.**

DOG DEN

The room speaks volumes—dog-eared volumes— of a city couple's passion for canines. In the course of a year of casual collecting, it went from a TV room with baseball memorabilia to a full-fledged dog den. Most of the items were found at the sprawling flea market that comes to life every weekend at Sixth Avenue and 26th Street in Manhattan.

While only a handful of dealers anywhere specialize solely in canine antiquities and collectibles, a number of the operatives at the New York flea market consistently carry a few dog things. One Sunday, the couple felt as if they had scored a bonanza, finding within minutes of their arrival both a Victorian footstool and an old hooked rug, each with a winning canine head on it. But even on slow days they seldom return home without something under wraps, such as the

Above: **When the lightbulb, sold as a novelty item in the 1920s, is switched on, the filament glows in the image of a Scottie.** *Right:* **Behind the sleeper sofa, with its array of needlepoint and chenille dog pillows, the bookshelves are turned out with small paintings and prints of bloodhounds and terriers and a collection of carved dog bookends in brass, bronze, iron, and stone.**

Above left: **A jumble of bookends, old postcards, and dog photos turns a bookshelf into a visual kennel.** *Above:* **Tramp art frames enclose an old print and a newly commissioned portrait of the owner's dog.** *Far left:* **Old wire dog muzzles are stowed on a shelf below a primitive print of two dogs.** *Left:* **Cut-paper renderings, fashionable in Victorian times, imitated needlework designs. The milk glass picture hangers, dating from the 1860s, are painted with dog portraits.** *Opposite, clockwise from top left:* **Taking a break in Washington Square Park; first aid kits for pets, a popular British import carried by the old Abercrombie & Fitch in the 1930s and 1940s; and an elegant metal dog bed, complete with bed spring, with a patent date of 1932.** *Following pages:* **American-made feed bowls from the 1930s to the 1950s.**

wire dog muzzles they stumbled on in a box of wood toys. Now the muzzles lend their sculptural quality to a tabletop in the den.

Utilitarian objects such as dog bowls, the couple discovered, were easy to find and, if chips and cracks in them could be ignored, relatively inexpensive to collect. One late-19th-century dog bowl made in England came with the steep price tag of $175, but the vast majority of the bowls, American made and dating from the 1930s through the 1950s, cost from $5 to $95. Some are still serviceable; others have sprung leaks but can be used to hold car keys and pocket change. Still others serve no better purpose than to provide an assemblage of earthy colors to a room.

As canine books and pictures, rugs and pillows, collars and doorstops multiplied, the Boston Red Sox collection belonging to the man of the house was politely nudged out of the den in the city and into his office in the country—nearer, anyway, to Fenway Park. Replacing the autographed photograph of Ted Williams in the den is a 19th-century watercolor rendering of dog's best friend—the flea.

Among the most unusual pieces of folk art in the den is a pair of electric lightbulbs, "manufactured as novelty items in the late 1920s," with filaments made in the embossed shapes of a Scottie and a schnauzer. Installed in a lamp or sconce and plugged in, the shapes soon glow bright red, showing off all the details of each feisty breed. "We really became intrigued by the fact that dogs had been such a popular motif in almost any product line you could imagine."

Opposite: **One corner of the den shows off a collection of pencil drawings, prints, and watercolors from the late 19th and early 20th centuries.** *Below:* **Above the Boston terrier garden ornament and doorstop is an entomologically correct watercolor of the common dog flea, painted in the late 19th century.**

PART THREE

DOGS
in the
Country

In the Company of Newfies is a poignant, richly detailed, and sometimes humorous account of a year that novelist Rhoda Lerman and her husband devoted almost entirely to the breeding, raising, and showing of prize Newfoundlands, a breed she had fallen in love with, quite by accident, a decade earlier. Early in the book, Lerman effectively sums up the impact of a litter of eight newborn Newfies on the couple's heirloom country house in upstate New York:

My once lovely house is a dogs' house now. City friends no longer come for elegant country weekends. Victorian society architect Stanford White would roll over in his grave if he knew what was going on below his vaulted ceilings, arched doorways, leaded glass, Doric columns. This was not his intention. I suspect the house smells. I no longer know. Hairs rise and float from furniture as we move past. Each week we wipe caked slime from the gorgeous woodwork, pawprints from the doors and floors, vacuum hair from carpets. . . . Even though stones fill kennel areas and the approach to the house, dogs absorb mud, puppies make mud, dig holes, spill water. Neighbors don't drop in any longer. A playwright comes for lunch, looks us over in our sweatpants and dirty jeans, our stained sneakers, tells us we look as if we're camping out in someone else's mansion. We do not fit the background. We've given precise meaning to the cliché, "gone to the dogs."

But the experience of the Lermans was hardly typical of people with dogs in the country. The Newfoundland, famous for serving fishermen, for rescuing children in choppy seas, and for acting as the loyal companion of Lord Byron, is one of the largest of canine breeds, weighing up to 150 pounds as an adult male. To raise a litter of Newfie puppies requires something of a heroic effort and is necessarily hard on the furnishings and the social life.

For most country dwellers, however, a dog is as easy to live with as a flock of songbirds. With at least one dog per pickup truck, the canine population in the rural countryside is actually on the rise, even though many of the traditional tasks of dogs on farms and ranches have been eliminated or downsized. In fact, people have turned to dogs for companionship in the country in almost as large numbers as they have in city and suburbs. Dogs commonly tag along with their owners to work or to the store, and they bring their cheerful spirit, curiosity, and energy to public events like Memorial Day parades, Fourth of July celebrations, county fairs, flea markets, and harvest festivals. Somehow the presence of dogs infuses the events of small-town America with an innocence reminiscent of Currier & Ives and Norman Rockwell.

open, the terriers sprint hell-for-leather after the tail, which is pulled along the ground by a machine located on the other side of the finish line. Some of the dogs carom off each other as they hurdle the 8- to 18-inch obstacles on the 150-foot course. The first dog through the small hole in the pile of straw bales at the finish is declared the winner. Winners of the heats then compete for the title.

Nothing ever goes quite as planned with Jack Russells, however. Sometimes a terrier escapes its handler before the start, catches the tail, and does everything it can to keep it. There are collisions and pileups on the course and at the finish line. Meanwhile, on the sidelines for each heat, nonparticipating Jack Russells can barely be contained by the owners, their desire to join in the action is so keen.

The race elicits the behavior Jack Russells were bred for in the first place—to go down a hole after a fox and, once there, not to catch the fox but to chase it out of the den by creating as much havoc as possible. The result is a breed of dog small enough to get through a foxhole, bold and brassy enough to face down the snapping teeth of an angry prey, and smart enough not to get caught. Or, as one horseman who has long been surrounded by these little terriers maintains, "If it's small, tough, and doesn't come when you call it, then it's a Jack Russell."

The hunting heritage of Jack Russells originated in foxhunting country in England in the middle to late 1800s. The dog was developed as a breed by one Jack Russell, a reputedly hard-drinking, hard-riding man of the cloth, and its special

Below: **On the scent of animal fur laid down for purposes of the race, Jack Russells demonstrate their natural dedication to the hunt right out of the starting gate.**
Opposite, clockwise from top left: **The kennel at Windermere Farm, owned by Linda Cowasjee, has produced numerous champion Jack Russell terriers; Cowasjee (on bench) with two of her dogs and a friend; purveyors at the Virginia Hunt Cup sell everything from BMWs to Victorian stickpins; by midrace, the outcome is still up in the air.**

Below left: **A young spectator at the Jack Russell terrier race.** *Below right:* **Windermere Farm's memorabilia of the breed.**
Bottom: **Begun in 1922, the Virginia Gold Cup race at Great Meadow near Plains, Virginia, inspires tailgate parties of all descriptions every year, affording racegoers the chance to socialize, to see and be seen, and to show off their colorful attire.**

Below left: **The Gold Cup has been described as "the Kentucky Derby, run over four miles of gently indulating terrain, with thirteen breast-high fences to be jumped twenty-three times."** *Below right:* **A walking stick of horn with a Jack Russell handle.** *Bottom:* **Pins collected by Linda Cowasjee over years of work with her favorite breed.**

affinity for horses continues to this day. In riding to Virginia's Piedmont Hunt, Linda Cowasjee has carried Jacks with her on horseback, tucked in a kind of canine Snugli, for use if a fox needed to be bolted (unharmed) from some earthen den so that the hunt could continue.

"It likes nothing better than to run and hunt," says Linda. "I see to it that my dogs get to run five or six miles a day in our paddock. They do not do well unless they can indulge in some form of hunting, whether it's chasing squirrels or killing voles. That's why they are not a dog for everyone."

Linda encountered her first Jack Russell as a youngster riding horses on Long Island. "A man who owned one of the stables where I rode had brought a dog over from England to keep down the vermin in his barn. At that time there were hardly any Jacks in this country," she recalls. "My first impression was that this little dog had no concept of his size. He was afraid of nobody."

About a dozen dogs occupy her kennels at Windermere Farm at any one time. Newcomer puppies and older dogs, like fourteen-year-old Quill, a tired but noble veteran of the Jack Russell wars, get to live with the Cowasjees and their parrot, Gypsy, in the main house.

"Gypsy whistles at them, calls for them by name, and orders them around, imitating my voice," Linda relates. "It can be pretty funny when I'm sitting with dinner guests and they hear what sounds like me crying out, 'Go and lie down, Sparkle!' or 'Be quiet, Wasp!' On the other hand," she adds, "Gypsy can get on your nerves. She imitates every appliance in the house. Living with her is like 'noise of the week.'"

Opposite: **At the close of the race, owners work quickly to scoop up their entries, before, as sometimes happens, one or more terriers decide to head off in other directions.** *Below:* **With dogs no taller than 15 inches high, not even three's a crowd.**

HUMANE SOCIETY

For a dog whose name was picked from a hat, Pookie has done pretty well for himself, with homes he can call his own in New York, Paris, and Sharon, Connecticut.

"He's led quite a life," says Carolyne Roehm, fashion designer and lifestyle author, of her beloved seventeen-year-old West Highland white terrier, one of six dogs underfoot at Weatherstone, her country estate. "He's been in *Vanity Fur* (the parody), in my catalog, and in ads. Early one morning I was walking him in New York. A fashion photographer, driving by, leaned out of his van window and cried, 'Look, that's Pookie!' What can I say? He's a dog with a face that could launch a thousand ships."

Carolyne first came upon Pookie in a store window, of all places.

Above and right: **At Carolyne Roehm's country home in Connecticut, six dogs, among them Annie, a two-year-old cairn terrier, lead the proverbial Life of Riley. A collection of English Regency and Irish cut crystal urns and an 1848 portrait,** *Billy, Holt Castle's Faithful Watch,* **grace the dining room at Weatherstone.** *Following pages:* **In the living room, fresh bouquets from the garden mingle with 18th-century Delft and 19th-century Chinese and "Yesterday Taiwan" porcelains, setting off a painting depicting a lull in the action of an English foxhunt.**

"I was coming home from work one snowy night in the city," she relates. At the time she was married to financier Henry Kravis and working as a design assistant for Oscar de la Renta. "Working such long hours in the fashion business, I was never at home, but Henry's children badly wanted a dog, and when I passed this dog store, there he was. My friends were horrified that I had gotten a dog in a shop and not from a breeder of pedigree. But Pookie had such a look in his eye that I knew he was the right dog for us."

Other dogs were added to the menagerie at Weatherstone, starting with two

Labrador retrievers, Nabisco and Christie (named in honor of a huge business deal negotiated by Kravis). When Stoneleigh, a black Scottish terrier, arrived, Pookie went into a funk for six months, refusing to have anything to do with the Scottie. "But then they became buddies," Carolyne notes. When Annie, a cairn terrier, arrived one Christmas Eve, as a present for Carolyne, it was Stoneleigh's turn to have his nose out of joint. "But now they all play and play and play," she declares.

All the dogs stayed with Carolyne following her divorce in 1993, and yet another was added: a twelve-year-old German shepherd named Ike. "I inherited him from

This page and opposite: **Terriers real and imagined occupy a variety of perches at Weatherstone. While Annie, Pookie, and Stoneleigh, the Scottie, are discouraged from running amok in the owner's sumptuous flower gardens, they enjoy virtual free rein inside the house.**

a friend who had rescued him from an abusive home in Kansas City," she explains. Skinny and afflicted with heartworm when he arrived, Ike was nursed back to health and now, she says, "is the sweetest dog and the most protective, especially of Annie and me. He won't let anyone near the house that he doesn't know."

While the Labs spend their days hanging out with the horses in Carolyne's stables, the terriers are in and out of the house and the many gardens that grace the grounds. "If I make twenty trips to the garden and back," says Carolyne, "Pookie and the girls make them with me." Her first book, *A Passion for Flowers*, draws on a love for gardening that is as intense as her love for dogs. "If I see my animals do something charming or find a huge dahlia that's a luscious red color, I physically feel the surge in my heart, like it's getting bigger."

Growing up in rural Misssouri, Carolyne had a succession of dogs, from Bobo, a boxer, to Chumley, "a little prissy Maltese that we all fell for." Today she misses her dogs when she travels between her houses, in connection with a book on entertaining she is preparing and a new catalog business, selling home accessories under the name Home by Carolyne Roehm. Returning to the dogs is always a special pleasure.

"They go crazy the minute they hear my voice, and then there are lots of tummy rubs," she observes, adding more reflectively, "They make me smile, make me laugh out loud. I love watching them play and I have all these goofy pictures of them. I basically like dogs better than people! That's why I've always said, 'The house can burn, but save my dogs.'"

Below: **An old iron dog guards the dining room hearth.** *Bottom:* **With canines on hands, the breakfast room is a cheerful place to work.** *Opposite:* **Ike was rescued from an abusive situation and, with time, has been made to feel right at home.**

A COUNTRY VET

When Dr. Fred Cesana opened his veterinary clinic in Plainville, Connecticut, in 1975, he wanted to soften the clinical look of its waiting room and examining rooms with decor that would have eye appeal yet make sense, stylistically, for a practice devoted to small animals.

As a lifelong collector who was familiar with the flotsam and jetsam of the world of flea markets and auction houses, Fred quickly found his focus for the clinic. "I started collecting cabinets that had been used to sell veterinary patent medicines in general stores early in the century," he relates. "In the 1970s, these things were fairly easy to find, and most of them were not that expensive. It was fun to look for them, and it also turned out to be a good investment for the business."

From about 1900 into the 1930s, there were numerous manufac-

Above: **Dr. Fred Cesana checks out a two-year-old English setter named Buster in his Connecticut clinic.** *Right:* **Artifacts of early veterinary medicine, nutrition, and care form the core of a collection that Dr. Cesana has assembled over the years.**

turers of remedies for whatever ailed horses, cows, goats, sheep, and, a bit later, dogs, too. Many were regional, serving rural populations in an age when almost every small-town family had a cow. Others, like Dr. Daniels and the International Stock Food Co., were nationally known brand names. The cabinets were used to display colic cures and gall salves for stomachaches and harness sores in farm animals. When dogs began to be treated as pets, worm medicines and flea soaps were added to the product line. Some cabinets had glass doors, while others were embellished with vivid graphic images, often of domestic animals.

"The old cabinets looked right at home in our clinic," Fred says, especially after he added to the walls Humane Society posters and other canine art of the same era, which he had collected concurrently. "I'm more of a visual person than some people," he notes, "so the things I collect I like to see."

Besides the vintage veterinary artifacts, Dr. Cesana has amassed impressive collections of baskets and blue-decorated stoneware. "Collecting for me started out as a diversion from practicing veterinary medicine," he says, "but as it went on, I came back to collecting things with animals on them." He notes that stoneware makers of the mid-19th century depicted dogs in sharply contrasting styles. A butter churn in Fred's collection, made in about 1860 in Rochester, New York, bears a detailed rendering of a dog that is clearly a King Charles spaniel, while a jug made at about the same time in Bennington, Vermont, is painted with

Below left: **Canine medications and dog care treatises from the 1920s were an outgrowth of the treatments veterinarians first developed for farm animals.** *Below right:* **The waiting room at Old Canal Veterinary Clinic offers the latest in veterinary science as well as glimpses into the care and feeding of the dogs of the past, including a Dr. A. C. Daniels veterinary medicine cabinet and an Old Trusty dog food barrel.** *Opposite:* **Posters circulated by the Connecticut Humane Society in the 1930s reminded people to look after the welfare of horses, dogs, and other animals, especially in hot weather. An old cat carrier and a bulldog advertising Clayton Dog Remedies are on the bench.**

a more abstracted, "folky" version of a dog that could belong to one of many breeds.

Dr. Cesana grew up on a Connecticut farm that had a few animals of practically every kind, including a collie cross named Daisy who indirectly led him to his choice of career. "I had a nightmare when I was seven years old that Daisy went next door and had her head bitten off," he recalls. "The dream, I think, was brought on by some grotesque story I'd seen in *Life* about a Russian scientist who had grafted a second head onto a dog for an experiment. Anyway, the next morning I asked my parents what we would do if Daisy got hurt and needed to be fixed. They said, 'Take her to a veterinarian.' From that day on, that's what I wanted to be."

After studying at the University of Connecticut and Michigan State, Fred opened Old Canal Veterinary Clinic, which has since expanded to a second location, in Bristol, Connecticut, and a staff of seven vets. Since World War II, there has been a steady rise in veterinary practices devoted exclusively to pets, and significant changes in the way people relate to their dogs.

"Back when Dr. Daniels was sold in country stores, dogs lived in the barn or out in the yard," Dr. Cesana observes. "We began letting them into the kitchen or den in the 1960s and 1970s. By the 1990s they were in our bedrooms."

While some of his older clientele want only minimal treatment for their animals, just the shots needed to avoid a fine, more and more people insist on giving their pets almost the same level of health care they expect for themselves. "Pets have become very important to owners, almost as if they are their children," Dr. Cesana says. "One survey reports that many people feel closer to their dogs than to their

Below, left to right: **A rare stoneware butter churn with canine scene, made by W. Clark & Co., Rochester, New York; a letter from the Old Trusty Dog Food Company to a would-be customer in the 1930s; Dr. Cesana's practice extends beyond dogs and cats to birds and reptiles.**

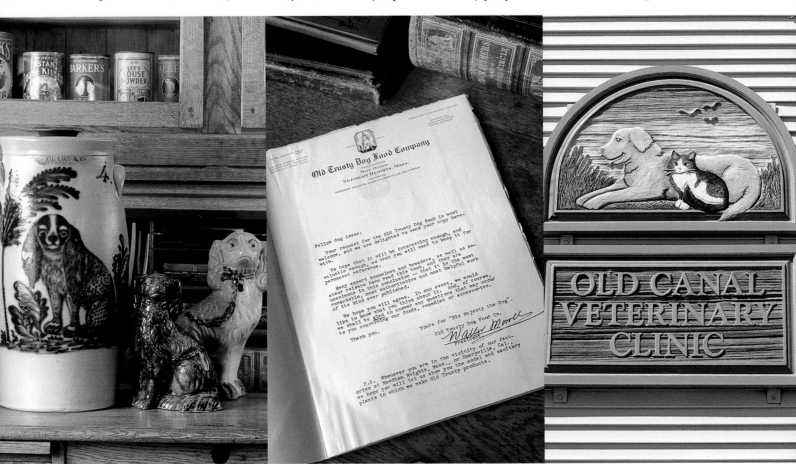

spouses! We even recommend grief counselors for some clients when their pets become ill and die, because the loss is so devastating for them."

The emotional connection to canines is most noticeable in people who own dogs primarily for companionship, and also in those who adopt dogs who have been abused or neglected. Sporting dogs used primarily for pointing, hunting, or retrieving may be admired for their traits in the field but traditionally have been relegated to the kennel when the hunt is done. Increasingly, however, even dogs bred for special purposes outdoors are being welcomed into the home.

When Dr. Cesana's uncle took him hunting as a boy, an orange-and-white English setter named Jill came along to point birds for them. In more recent years he has hunted pheasant with springer spaniels and Labrador retrievers, but presently he's back to English setters, Cassie and George by name, and he is happy with them. "Setters have a reputation for hunting in one county while you're in the next," he observes, "but Cassie stays in close and holds a bird on point beautifully, and George, her son, is fairly reliable when he's with his mother in the field."

Fred's most recent collecting goal is to find old photographs showing dogs with their owners. "People had to think a lot of their pets to include them in these old tintypes and cabinet cards," he observes. "That human-animal bond is what I like to see captured. It's hard to find early photos with clear expressions on the faces of the dogs, because the animals tended to move during the long exposures that were required for photography back then, but they do exist. The best ones I hope to blow up and put on the walls in the clinic."

Below: **Stoneware painted with dogs stand amid old shipping crates for horse and cattle powders. The four-gallon jug was made by J. & E. Norton, Bennington, Vermont, in about 1854.**

MR. STEWART'S CHESHIRE FOXHOUNDS

"Poor old car," Nancy Penn Smith Hannum sighs as she guides her battered blue Jeep Wagoneer through a rocky creek in the bottom of a field, her Jack Russell terrier, Journey, balancing on the top of the backseat, "but as long as it runs, that's all that matters to me."

It is not exactly the vehicle one expects to see driven by the wife of a federal judge, John B. Hannum; the niece of a governor and diplomat, Averell Harriman; and the granddaughter of a Wall Street whiz and railroad magnate, Edward H. Harriman. But the hunt is the thing for Nancy Hannum, not the trappings, and it has been thus for more than half a century.

Above and right: **Tributes to foxhounds abound in the house and kennels of a hunt founded in 1914 by Plunket Stewart in Unionville, Pennsylvania, and passed along in 1948 to his stepdaughter, Mrs. John B. Hannum, who has been running it ever since. As Mrs. Hannum's huntsman, Joseph Cassidy is in charge of the hounds and their daily activities.**

When I meet with Mrs. Hannum, master of Mr. Stewart's Cheshire Foxhounds, one of the country's most venerable hunts, in Unionville, Pennsylvania, she is following horses and hounds one early fall day in so-called cubbing season. This is only a run-up to the real hunt season, but even on a bad scenting day, experts say, a good pack of hounds will never take their noses off the ground. On this morning there are signs that the outing is productive, for when she puts on the brakes at the next rise and leans out the car window, she hears her English foxhounds "speaking" in a clamor of voices, and the sound of an English hunting horn, blown by her huntsman to encourage the hounds. "They are certainly on a fox," she declares.

A horsewoman of legendary courage and skill, Mrs. Hannum no longer rides to hounds now that, in her seventies, her numerous riding injuries have caught up with her. But she is still deeply involved in every other aspect of the hunt, from overseeing the care, feeding, and breeding of the hounds to combating any threat to the openness of her hunt country. One friend has written that "she has exercised a sort of overlordship in matters of land management that often has conflicted with 20th century notions of personal property rights." In other words, do not try to build something where it is not wanted. One concession the hunt did make was to allow Alfred Hitchcock to film the hunt scenes for *Marnie* at Unionville, but when the movie was released in 1964, Mrs. Hannum pronounced it "not his best."

Foxhounds are not pets; they are bred and trained to live as a pack and to hunt foxes tirelessly, yet Mrs. Hannum treats her hounds as well as she does her beloved Journey. Their kennels are a stately canine Hilton built in the 1930s of native stone with two carved foxes on pillars framing the entrance. Inside are two spacious, well-ventilated lodging rooms for dogs (the males), and two for bitches. For hunting, Mrs. Hannum prefers bitches—"so cheery and quick and more responsive." The hounds sleep on benches made of heat-absorbing cement and bedded down with hay. Each lodging room has its own automatically refilled water bowl, heated in the winter so that it never freezes.

A communal feed room, with a large metal trough running the length of it, is positioned on one side of the kennel. Mrs. Hannum's hunt staff retrieves old horses with injuries, or cattle that have died on nearby farms, to butcher and mix the meat with commercial dog feed, gravy, and water to make into a porridge.

When Mrs. Hannum catches up with the hunt, the horses and hounds are spent, but huntsman Joe Cassidy, her second-in-command, is smiling. He rides over to Mrs. Hannum and leans out of his English saddle to regale her with the details.

Typically, Mrs. Hannum begins her day at around 5:30 A.M. She meets with staff in a makeshift office in a horse barn down the hill from the kennels. Surrounded by hunt trophies and a jumble of ribbons from foxhound trials, she reviews dates and

Below: **An 1899 portrait by the English artist John Emms shows foxhounds and one terrier in a lodging room.** *Opposite, left:* **Four paintings of hounds by Cuthbert Bradley, dating from 1933, lend canine character to a downstairs hallway at Brooklawn.** *Right:* **The portrait of Mr. Stewart's Cheshire Foxhounds was painted by F. B. Voss in 1948, the year Nancy Hannum took over as master of foxhounds.**

Below, left to right: **Among the rogue's gallery of English hounds is Mrs. Hannum and her terrier, Traveler, and an objet d'art in her house.** *Bottom left:* **During informal hunting of young foxes during late summer and early fall, hounds go out as early as possible in the warm weather, usually around 7:00 A.M.** *Bottom right:* **In the kennel yard for young hounds, the daughter of a staff member takes a riding lesson. Adjacent yards separately house male hounds, referred to as dogs, and bitches.**

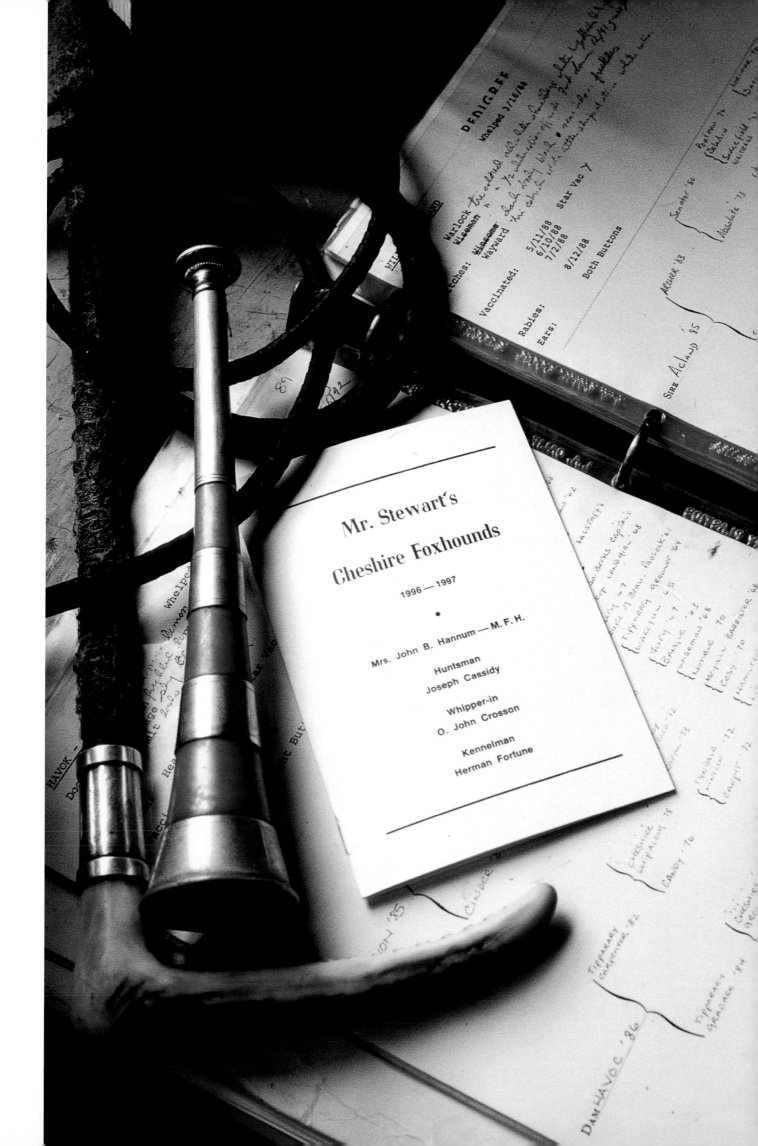

Mr. Stewart's

Cheshire Foxhounds

1996 — 1997

•

Mrs. John B. Hannum — M.F.H.

Huntsman
Joseph Cassidy

Whipper-in
O. John Crosson

Kennelman
Herman Fortune

schedules in several ledgers filled with her barely decipherable longhand script. Her day ends around 6:00 P.M. with a hot bath and supper at nearby Brooklawn, her family's ancestral brick home, which is filled with paintings and other reminders of the hunt—and also with the occasional bat, which she and the housekeeper smite with badminton rackets stationed inconspicuously but conveniently around the house. Sadly, Judge Hannum, having suffered a stroke, is confined to his room with nurses around the clock.

As Mrs. Hannum and Joe Cassidy conclude their conversation, Joe and one of his whippers-in gather up the hounds for the return to the kennel, calling some by name: Parson, Acrobat, Minstrel, Rector, Racer, Caveat, Rambler. . . . Foxhounds are among the most stoic and soldierly breeds of canine and appear so especially when they are hacking home. Sun breaks through a shred of clouds. Mrs. Hannum stands in the dappled light, leaning against her Jeep, taking in the passing scene.

Her beaming face, tanned and deeply lined by a lifetime of hunts in all manner of weather, looks up at the riders as they pass her, one at a time, and offer her "good night," the traditional hunt farewell, even though it is not yet nine in the morning (some will rush home to change into business attire and head for work), with deference and feeling:

Below: **Mrs. Hannum, flanked by a bronze sculpture of a hound at Brooklawn and the carved stone foxes at the entrance to her kennels, built of native fieldstone after the original building burned to the ground in 1930.** *Opposite:* **Precise records ensure that the hounds of the Unionville hunt are bred to produce animals with vigorous hunting instincts; fresh English foxhound bloodlines are also brought into the kennels from time to time.**

"Thank you, Mrs. Hannum, good night."

"Good night, Mrs. Hannum."

"Mrs. Hannum, thank you, ma'am, and good night."

She replies to every rider by name, with a smile and a particular radiant beauty all her own, until the last is gone.

DOG DAY AFTERNOON

For more than half a century, the Virginia Foxhound Club has conducted an annual show for the judging of America's premier American and English foxhounds. The hound show, a traditional Memorial Day weekend fixture drawing more than 800 entries from foxhunts all over the country, is now staged on the sweeping lawn of Morven Park, a 1,200-acre estate outside the town of Leesburg in Loudon County, Virginia. Formerly the home of Governor Westmoreland Davis of Virginia, the stately Greek Revival mansion with its columned portico makes an appropriate backdrop for an event conducted with Old Dominion formality and pomp. The north wing houses a collection of paintings, bronzes, and other artifacts portraying famous hounds, huntsmen, and hunts in North America, the oldest item being a gracefully curved hunting horn owned by Colonial Governor Samuel Ogle of Maryland in 1731.

Above and right: **The annual Virginia Foxhound Club show, now held at Morven Park, has been a fixture in hunt circles for more than half a century. Huntsmen and their packs come from all over the country.**

Above: **Like dogs at purebred shows, foxhounds are judged against a written standard for the breed, including height; American foxhounds measure 21 to 25 inches at the withers.**

With more than eighty classes to be judged, the daylong event unfolds slowly, culminating in the awarding of the William W. Brainard Jr. Perpetual Cup for the Grand Champion Foxhound of the Show. American foxhounds, English foxhounds, and crossbreeds of either sex are eligible for the top award. American foxhounds stand at 22 to 25 inches at the withers for males, 21 to 24 inches for females. English foxhounds are larger in bone than their American cousins but similar in temperament: smart, stolid, and comfortable in the company of other animals. In recent years, crossbreds have triumphed over the English and American champion foxhounds at the show.

When Live Oak Hostess, a female crossbred from Monticello, Florida, won the top prize in 1998, its exhibitor, joint master of foxhounds Martin Wood III, called it "a marvelous stop along the path of a breeding program. I love my hounds and I'm real pleased, but the important thing is that they hunt so well as a pack of hounds. The bottom line is that they function as a unit."

Albert Poe, one of Virginia's most respected huntsmen and foxhound breeders, echoes that sentiment. "You've got to breed your own pack, breed them close enough and work them close enough that they all begin to think alike and act alike," he says. "If I holler once, I want every hound to hear it."

DOG DAY AFTERNOON

Poe spent twenty years as huntsman for Mrs. A. C. Randolph's Piedmont Fox Hounds, and since 1980 has handled a superb pack for the Middleburg Hunt. Frequently enlisted as a judge of hounds in the show ring, he says he looks beyond physical appearance and stature to more intangible qualities, which he gauges by the "look in his eye—whether he'll look at you or cower when you go near him, whether he's proud, likes to be touched." He observes, "A hound has to be a proud animal, a strong animal, and be able to get along with people and other hounds."

It often takes a decade or more to develop a pack of forty hounds that act like one in the field. Well in advance of breeding season, Poe and other huntsmen like him go through the books on all their bitches and dogs, making notes and comparing everything that will influence a match—bloodlines, behavior traits, physical problems.

Poe advocates limiting the hounds in a pack to one strain. "If you've got American hounds, English hounds, and crossbred hounds all in the same pack," he says, "you're not going to have the same control over them, or get the same reaction out of one that you will out of another. You can't use the same tone of voice, whip control, or horn control on three different kinds of hounds."

The American hound does not respond well to prolonged whipping on but will do anything if treated fairly. The English hound also responds to encouragement but has to be handled a little more firmly than his American cousin.

Above and below: **Kennels for visiting packs, often festooned with leashes and other gear, are kept clean and dry for the duration of the show.** *Following pages:* **A hound's-eye view of the action during show weekend.**

"If you want them to act as a unit, the best group of hounds you'll ever see are ideally brothers and sisters," Poe asserts. However, males and females do not hunt well together, "so you try to have a lot of hounds by the same stud dog. They're more likely to be of the same mind and disposition because they are blood-related."

The type of country to be hunted dictates another consideration for breeding. "If you've got big, wide-open country, you can have a hound who can run on, because you can ride to stay with him," says Poe. "But if you're hunting a lot of woodland and rough country, you want a hound with a good nose rather than great speed, and the ability to stay on the line of the fox and keep tracking it until it comes out."

Reflecting on a profession that requires long hours in all kinds of weather, and constant physical exertions, Poe says, "I could probably do other jobs that would pay me more than I can make as a huntsman, but no other line of work would give me the thrill of hearing a pack of hounds open on a fox that's just up early in the morning. The woods sound like they're coming apart when you hear forty hounds really doing their job."

Poe believes a good huntsman should even be ready to make the ultimate

Opposite: **The slow pace of the Virginia Foxhound Show provides plenty of opportunities for handlers to relax with their entrants.**
Below, left to right: **Prizes are awarded in a wide range of categories, but only one hound merits the designation Grand Champion; many showgoers sport the emblems of other events and associations; judges scrutinize foxhounds for how closely they conform to the written standard in general appearance and myriad other factors such as gait, coat, and temperament.**

sacrifice when it comes to his hounds. "I get along with just about every dog I meet," he says. "Now, if a dog wants to mark his territory for you and your leg happens to be the corner post, you're going to have to put up with wet socks!"

The Virginia Foxhounds Show closes in a much more decorous fashion, with a melodic horn-blowing contest among huntsmen. Competitors blow four calls: moving off, gone away, gone to ground, and going home. In that way, the biggest hound show in America ends on a high note.

FOR THE
LOVE OF DOGS

Lucinda Lang calls Tenants Harbor "springer heaven" because this town on the pristine Saint George peninsula on the coast of Maine is surrounded by towering stands of spruce, fir and tamarack, rolling hayfields, and rocky coastline—the ideal mixed-use habitat for her three spirited English springer spaniels, Isabelle, Jack, and Yvonne. "To have happy springers in the house," Cindy says of her silken-coated trio, "they need lots of exercise outside the home—not just walks but all-out romps."

The Lang family, originally from New Orleans, has been coming to Tenants Harbor since Cindy was a child, always accompanied by their dogs, which tended to be mixed-breeds from the pound or from some neighbor's accidental litter. It was not until Cindy went off to the University of Denver that she upgraded the family's taste in canines to purebred spaniels. She and a boyfriend happened to bring home a

Above and right: **The road sign, handpainted by a young friend, Jonathan Mort, points visitors to Cindy Lang's tranquil retreat by the sea.**

springer puppy named Sappho from a breeder on a Colorado ranch. It was the boyfriend's idea, but the dog became Cindy's love, and she has been stuck on the breed ever since. Sappho (despite her name) begat Binky, who begat Winnie, who begat Samantha, who begat the legendary Trout.

"When Trout came down with cancer at age twelve, I was devastated," Cindy recalls. "Trout was the kind of dog who got postcards from casual acquaintances, people admired him so much. I remember telling friends about the diagnosis, and coming home and finding a freshly painted watercolor of Trout on my icebox, drawn from life that afternoon by Anna B. McCoy, a friend of mine who is an artist. So I cried some more."

In fact, chemotherapy helped the indomitable Trout enjoy another eighteen months with Cindy—much more quality time than the dog's vet had originally predicted. Like Johnny Appleseed, Cindy has sown her affection for springers far and wide, distributing puppies from new litters among friends and family. Occasionally she throws a reunion party for the clan, complete with painted springer masks and homemade springer biscuits. Her mother, Joel, had always given birthday parties for the dogs when they lived in New Orleans, inviting dogs of friends and neighbors over to make the occasion particularly festive, so Cindy is simply carrying on a family tradition. When one of her brothers, Bill, got married, his elaborately gowned bride appeared in a photo on the local society page with a wet springer in her lap. At the wedding reception, Bill stood up and confessed to

Below: **A collection of Staffordshire dogs, some originally belonging to Cindy's mother, adorns a rustic chest of drawers off the living room.** *Opposite:* **A drawing hung in the master bedroom, this one done by Jonathan Mort's sister, Kamissa, was presented as a gift to Cindy Lang after her dog, Isabelle, gave birth to a litter of six puppies in 1994.** *Following pages:* **In the light-filled living room, a barn scene of newborn pups was painted in oil in the 1940s by John McCoy and given to Cindy as a present by his widow, Anna B. McCoy. Another dog gift is the portrait of Trout, one of Cindy's favorite springers, hand-painted on fabric by friend Anne Morrill and made into a pillow.**

No room is off-limits to springer spaniels in the Lang household, one reason being that Cindy covers most of her upholstered furniture with washable slipcovers. *Top left:* When her beloved Trout came down with cancer, Cindy's friend Anna B. McCoy, Andrew Wyeth's niece, left an affectionate tribute to the dog on the refrigerator door; Cindy had it framed and hung it in her office. *Opposite, above:* The newly built seaside cottage was sited at a distance from the water so it would not intrude on the natural rugged beauty of the Maine coastline. *Below:* The dining area was designed with floor-length glass doors and windows on three sides.

the gathering, "We Langs are descended from a long line of springer spaniels."

Cindy's house, a sprawling shingled cottage complete with crow's nest and open porches, has the spartan, hardworking look of local grange halls from the early 1900s. Designed with her dogs in mind, the radiant-heated floors are made of poured, scored, and stained concrete. Windows were custom-made with very low sills so that the springers could easily look outside. There are also built-in dog portals at strategic locations, permitting Isabelle, the mother, and Jack and Yvonne, her offspring by two different dads, to come and go at will. Cindy enforces no particular rules about where the dogs go inside the house, either. "Basically, they can lounge anywhere they want—on the rugs, in the chairs and couches, on the beds—but if they are muddy or wet, they know enough not to test my patience," Cindy says. She takes the dogs with her on routine shopping trips and other errands, believing it to be important to make dogs part of every aspect of daily life, but when she is called away for longer periods, such as for meetings of the local land conservancy, in which she is active, Cindy simply houses them in a spacious dog den off the garage, originally the whelping room for her litters. It is furnished with blankets, chewies, toys, and a wall mural painted in acrylics by friend Will Cook. Part of the mural

Below, from left to right: **Willow, a sister of Yvonne, who also lives in Tenants Harbor; a memorial to one of Cindy's earlier springers, who loved being out on the rocks in the hot sun; and Yvonne, with her distinctive all-natural topknot.** *Opposite:* **A custom-made dog door gives Isabelle and the other spaniels of the house the ability to come and go as they desire.** *Following pages:* **A daylong springer spaniel party for Isabelle, Jack, Yvonne, and four of their closest relatives featured the staple attractions of any family reunion: a group photo, home-baked goodies, fun, games, and affection.**

depicts a bookshelf with fanciful titles, such as *Dogs Who Love Too Much, Afghan Style,* and *Animal Liberation.* The den also has its own portal leading to a large outdoor pen, in case the springers get bored with their books.

Cindy moved full-time to Maine in 1977 to manage rental properties for her family and other landowners on one of the few largely undeveloped coastal areas left in the state. They range from rustic cabins to saltwater farmhouses and classic

seaside cottages, and dogs are welcome in all of them. "With dogs of my own, I wouldn't have it any other way," she says, adding that "once in a while we have problems, but nothing so bad it can't be patched up. Dogs prone to digging, like beagles, tend to wreak havoc in our perennial gardens, and one summer two German shepherd mixes detected a mouse in one of our cottages and tore apart a wall trying to find it." Her own dogs are remarkably affable when canine strangers show up with families taking her rentals for a week or more.

Cindy's cottage blends seamlessly with land and sea as a result of meticulous plannning. "The last thing I wanted to do was disrupt the character of the property," says Lang, who consulted with a friend, land conservation planner Jerry Bley, on and off more than four years before settling on the building site, which allows the house to unobtrusively enjoy a sweeping panorama of water through the pines.

"Maine has seen so much insensitive use of coastal land in recent years," asserts Lang, an activist member of the Georges River Land Trust and the National Resources Council of Maine. Both groups work to save not only the things human settlers' esteem in Maine's open spaces, but those features and conditions that help to preserve many other life forms. "My family and I worked with Jerry to plan a conservation easement, locating my house near our antique Cape to purposely cluster the buildings so the open space would be conserved," she explains. "It is set back so that the nesting birds, the sea life, and all the critters that roam the shore can continue their activities undisturbed." The rest of the hundred acres have been left undeveloped for all visitors to enjoy—"kite flyers, cross-country skiers, hikers, picknickers," she adds, "and of course dog walkers."

When Cindy's father, Sam, died in October of 1989, the family decided that the burial would take place in the local Seaview Cemetery, and contacted a local sculp-

Below: **Most of Cindy Lang's long walks with her dogs end with a dip in the ocean, especially in summer.** *Opposite:* **A dog den off the garage, painted by a friend with a Maine seascape and a trompe l'oeil bookshelf, is full of creature comforts for the spaniels.**

tor, Steve Lindsay, to find and engrave a suitable headstone for them. That same week, an aged and ailing dog named Winnie, now blind, wandered away from home and failed to return. A raging thunderstorm came up overnight, making Winnie's prospects even dimmer and deepening Cindy's sense of loss. Beside herself, she finally asked for help from a rescue team, stationed at nearby Maine State Prison, which uses bloodhounds to find missing persons. It took the hounds almost twenty-four hours, but Winnie was finally located a few feet from the ocean's edge, alive but cold and very frightened. The dog had found refuge under a large granite stone near the

shore, not far from the house but shielded completely from human sight.

"Poor Winnie recovered from her ordeal," Cindy relates, "but what came as the surprise ending was that the next day Steve Lindsay went down on the beach, totally unaware of what had transpired there the day before, and picked for my father's headstone the very same stone that had given Winnie her shelter from the elements."

HERDING INSTINCTS

"The border collie is the only dog you can talk to and get an answer back," says Edgar Gould, a roundish small man with a pink face and flinty eyes who wears a John Deere cap as he leads his prize five-year-old border collie, Craig, to a pasture on his farm in Shelburne, Massachusetts.

On rare occasions, Mr. Gould, a renowned breeder and trainer of border collies, expertly demonstrates the art of sheepherding with his dogs for the public, but with traditional Yankee reserve, he places great store by his privacy. The Gould family's 18th-century brick house is surrounded by a catch-all of barn buildings, vacant chicken coops, sugar bush (a grove of sugar maples tapped every winter for their sweet sap), and rocky fields high on a ridge that the farmer describes as "one of the few quiet places left in the world."

Craig belongs to the predominant breed of herding dog in the

Above and right: **A well-trained border collie permits a single shepherd to control large herds of sheep, livestock, geese, or ducks, using only voice, whistle, and stick and arm commands.**

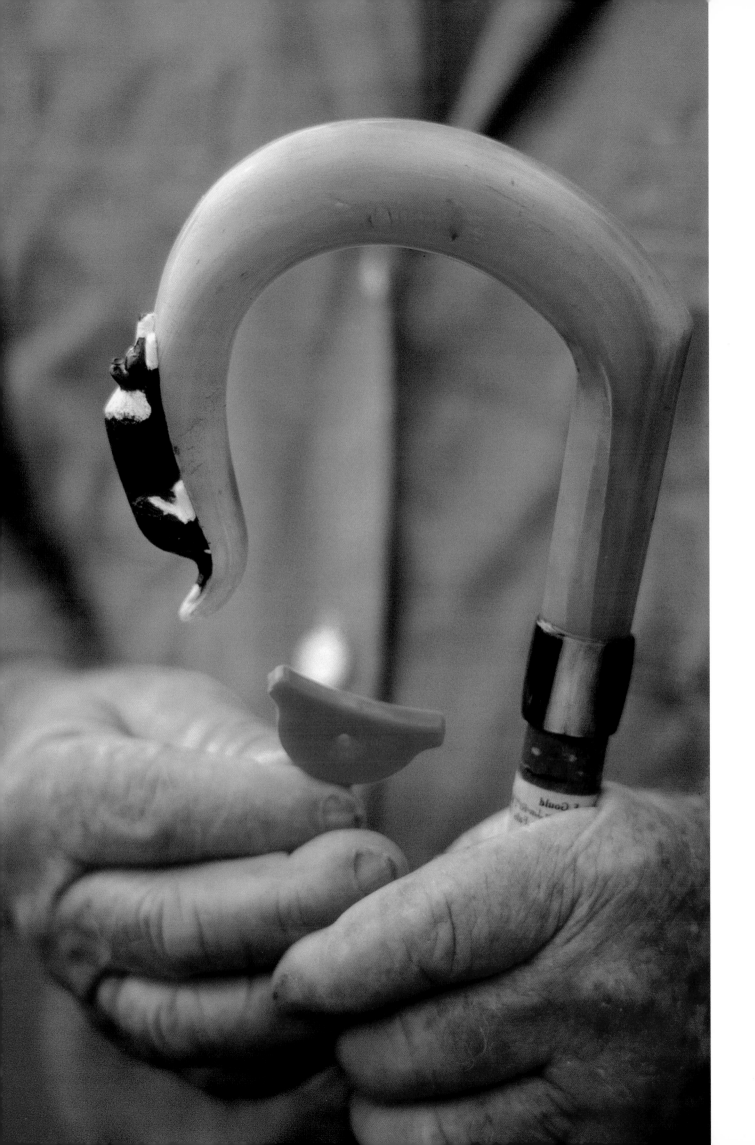

Western world. Border collies are found hard at work rounding up animals on nearly every livestock farm in Great Britain, where they originated in the early 19th century near the borders shared by England, Wales, and Scotland. In this country, the breed has found an unlikely but welcome new role on northeastern golf courses plagued by large populations of Canada geese, which had been fouling the grounds and waterways. Numerous golf clubs have successfully deployed border collies to chase the geese away.

The border collie is one of several dozen breeds for whom the act of gathering is practically a compulsion. From the low-set Welsh corgi to the shaggy Old English sheepdog, these breeds have worked successfully with herds of sheep and cattle, as well as goats, horses, geese, ducks, and chickens, for hundreds of years. Other notable herding dogs include the rough, smooth, and bearded collies, Shetland sheepdogs, German shepherds, briards, Australian cattle dogs (famous for canine longevity—twenty-nine years—and for controlling cattle in almost total silence), and the tough little Australian kelpies. Although some of these breeds are losing their popularity as herders, they are finding new roles as companions, show dogs, and service dogs.

Second in popularity to the border collie as a herder in the United States is probably the Australian shepherd. In fact, despite its name, this breed was developed completely in the United States beginning in the late 19th century. Forerunners of today's Aussies came to the western and northwestern territories as stock dogs for the Basque shepherds that accompanied the large herds of sheep then being

Below: **A successful trial ends with all the sheep safely penned.** *Opposite:* **Edgar Gould puts one of his prize border collies, Craig, through its paces on his farm in Shelburne, Massachusetts. "Good dogs are born," says Mr. Gould, one of the founders of the American Border Collie Association. "Better dogs are trained."**

imported from Australia. American farmers and ranchers began using them as well when they saw the agile, extremely intelligent, and hardworking dogs in action. Breeding was managed to foster working ability rather than appearance, and occasionally dogs of other herding breeds were bred into the line.

Through training, the shepherd, as "top wolf," teaches the herding dog to channel its hunting instincts into useful herding behaviors. Herding trials, sponsored by groups dedicated to maintaining the vigor and traditions of each herding breed, provide a chance for the public to see these dogs in action, usually with sheep, cattle, or geese, and to meet owners, trainers, and other admirers of these remarkable breeds. James Herriot captured the atmosphere of such events on a visit to a border collie trial in North Yorkshire, where he toiled as a veterinary surgeon, and consummate storyteller, for many decades. He describes the separate groups of human and canine participants as a culture of their own:

> *Groups of men, mainly competitors, stood around chatting as they watched. They were quiet, easy, bronzed men and as they seemed to be drawn from all social strata from prosperous farmers to working men their garb was varied; cloth caps, trilbies, deerstalkers or no hat at all; tweed jackets, stiff best suits, open-necked shirts, fancy ties, sometimes neither collar nor tie. Nearly all of them leaned on long crooks with handles fashioned from rams' horns.*
>
> *The dogs waiting their turn were tied up to a fence with a hedge growing over it. There were about seventy of them and it was rather wonderful to see that long row of*

Below: **Work done, a border collie takes five following a herding trial at Heritage Farm in Easthampton, Massachusetts.** *Opposite:* **Scenes from the annual Leaf Peeper Show at the Cambridge Saddle Club in Cambridge, New York, sponsored by the Working Australian Shepherd Club of Upstate New York. Such events often combine herding, obedience, and agility tests, with some classes open to all breeds.**

waving tails and friendly expressions. They were mostly strangers to each other but there wasn't even the semblance of disagreement, never mind a fight.

Back in Massachusetts, five horned Dorset sheep shift nervously in their pasture on the arrival of Mr. Gould and his dog. When the trainer blows a whistle, Craig takes off after the sheep and soon outflanks them, effectively cutting them off from a gate in the fence. "The gate is the pressure point," the farmer comments. Another whistle brings Craig to a sudden halt. The dog hunkers down near the sheep, eyeing his trembling miniflock with something approaching fervor. The "power" in the gaze of a border collie, a trademark of the breed, is a kind of secret weapon that permits the dog to control livestock without resorting to biting.

"See how his ears are cocked?" says Mr. Gould. "He's waiting for a signal." Moments later he whistles Craig away from the sheep and then, with the command, "Come by," brings him back to where he started. Nearly a dozen separate commands govern the behavior of a border collie in the field. When Mr. Gould says, "That'll do," the dog collapses in a satisfied heap.

"Do you pet him after he's done a good job?" the farmer is asked.

"Pet him?" says Mr. Gould incredulously. "When you get it all done, they know where they were doing right and where they were doing wrong. If he leaves the

Below left: **An Aussie waits for its owner to come back from registering for the day's competition at the Cambridge Saddle Club.** *Right:* **Owners are responsible for keeping their own dogs watered during a show.**

field smiling," he adds, nodding at Craig staring up at him, "that's what you look for. That's reward enough. And never mind feeding them tidbits. These dogs don't want anything but to do their work."

In fact, the trainer has serious reservations about all the attention border collies received following the movie *Babe,* the story of a pig who learns to herd sheep after befriending two border collies.

"You get the media interested in stories like how the border collie is the most intelligent dog in the world," he says, "and next thing you know, everyone wants a puppy." But Mr. Gould strongly disapproves of consigning action dogs, as he calls them, to life in confining city or suburban homes. "They're not able to do what they were born to do," he says.

On the way back from the exercise, the farmer passes another border collie confined to a fenced run. Much more striking in appearance than Craig, this dog has a handsome head and a broad white chest, but he is all show and no action.

"Duke is a big disappointment to me," says Mr. Gould, shaking his head. "He comes from the best of bloodlines, but he is very easily distracted. His mind is not on his business." Duke seems mildly chastised by the master's remark, for he flies atop his tin-roof doghouse, making a significant clatter.

"I like a good-looking dog," Mr. Gould declares, "but beauty is in the field."

Above: **The Harvest Moon Mania show, hosted by the Australian Shepherd Club of New England, set up its herding awards table in a stable convenient to the show grounds.** *Below:* **The owner of an Aussie puppy follows the herding trial action from the stands at Heritage Farm.**

A NOSE FOR ANTIQUES

Yes! to the 1870 Austrian handcut crystal necklace with the reverse-painted terrier on it. (Rare and unusual.)

No! to the set of three cast-aluminum chairs with painted images of a Colonial woman and Borzoi hound on the chairback. (A set takes four.)

Yes! to the pre–World War II Aerolux lightbulbs with filaments in the image of a Boston terrier and a pair of Scotties. (Folk industrial art at its best.)

No! to the mint-condition shoefly—a Colonial-era rocker for infants—with collies painted on it. (Too pricey at $600.)

So goes a day of shopping and assessing for Nancy Bergendahl, a dealer specializing in canine art and artifacts, at Brimfield, Massachusetts, one of America's largest flea markets. Nancy and her

Above and right: **Dogs real and imagined project star quality at open-air antiques shows like those produced three times a year at Brimfield, Massachusetts. The familiar Greyhound Bus Co. symbol was originally designed by Philadelphia-born Edwin Megargee, better known for his paintings of purebred and sporting dogs.**

husband, Peter, who has carved out a separate niche in old soda bottles, have been coming to Brimfield for more than three decades, both as dealers and buyers. They set up side by side in Sturveant's Field near the Congregational Church, and during lulls in the action, they scout the rest of the market.

"Buying is getting tougher," says Nancy. Her business, Henniker Kennel Company Antiques, is located in Henniker, New Hampshire, but she decamps for Brimfield with a selection of her eclectic merchandise for all three of its major annual shows, in May, July, and September, and also makes a few side trips to your better dog shows in the region. "Really good dog items are disappearing because more and more people are keeping the things they collect."

On the other hand, there are always new avenues to explore. "Antique photographs of dogs have become highly collectible," Nancy notes. "I have three or four collectors who value this medium as art." Two of her clients who deliver mail for the U.S. Postal Service happen to be avid collectors of dog tags—licenses for animals that by tradition regard the mailman as the enemy. "Dog licenses are small and easy to collect and display, so there's a market."

Nancy and Peter also have two wire-haired fox terriers, Topper, named after a gumball machine, and Patches, but they have given up on bringing them to Brimfield. "We had a Yorkie who was manageable," says Nancy, "but it was often too hot or too cold for her in the field. As for Topper, I remember taking him one time. Within three hours, he had dug twenty-eight holes and I had tripped twice on his leash."

Below: **Dealers who specialize in canine materials make one-stop shopping possible for dog collectors, but more eclectic holdings are as likely to yield a great find.**
Opposite: **Ephemera and old photographs, often found at flea markets and antiques shows, testify to the long-standing role of the dog in American culture.**

Girlsie. As she ascends a sweeping circular staircase hung with scores of paintings of dogs, the littermates, brother and sister, come pouring down the steps, scrapping and yapping all the way.

Sidestepping the dachshunds, she points to two 19th-century English paintings of spaniels on the wall and says dreamily, "I bought those from Pamela Harriman, years and years ago." A step later, another spaniel: "That one was a gift from Bill Blass . . . and the two miniatures next to it were painted by my friend Annette de la Renta."

Mrs. Astor has owned dogs and collected art and decorative objects dedicated to them practically all her life. She married her first husband, Dryden Kuser, at sixteen, in part because he promised her "all the dogs I wanted." After that marriage fell apart, she met Buddie Marshall while "beagling" in New Jersey—chasing rabbits on foot behind a pack of beagles for which she served as the whipper-in. During her twenty-year-long marriage to Marshall, Brooke went to work for *House and Garden* as a location editor and stylist. "A lady editor at Condé Nast's in those days wore a hat all day," she once recalled, "and could have her pet dog tied under her desk." With her charm and contacts in high places, she landed exclusive peeks into America's great houses for the magazine, such as Winterthur, Monticello, and Williamsburg, and a host of elegantly done private homes. When Buddie died in 1952, she was devastated, but before long another man came wooing: Vincent Astor, heir to one of America's great fortunes. He owned the St. Regis Hotel, *Newsweek,* and Ferncliff, a 3,500-acre estate on the Hudson River, among other things. They soon married, but the union ended with Vincent's death only five and a half years later.

Mrs. Astor inherited Ferncliff and took over the Vincent Astor Foundation and the philanthropic work that would become her enduring legacy. Over the next thirty-seven years, she presided over the dispersal of $195 million in the five boroughs of New York, funding youth services, public housing, and such cultural treasures as the Metropolitan Museum of Art and the New York Public Library (which had been founded by a grant by Astor family scion John Jacob Astor). She also championed innumerable smaller but no less important causes, such as the Animal Medical Center in Manhattan, where one of the foundation's grants, endowed in perpetuity, ensures that indigent people over sixty-five will always receive free care for their pets. That includes major medical treatment such as a pacemaker for an old dog with a weak ticker, or a back fusion operation for a dog with spinal sag (a condition to which dachshunds, one of Mrs. Astor's favorite breeds, are particularly susceptible).

After giving her visitor a tour of Holly Hill, Mrs. Astor returns to the entry hall, where several pieces of luggage and an attaché case have materialized, all with the monogram B.R.A. (The "R" is for Russell, her maiden name.) A Lincoln town car has pulled up to the front door. While the luggage is duly loaded into the car by the chauffeur and butler, Mrs. Astor reviews a note with several handwritten reminders, then opens a desk drawer and idly sorts through the mishmash of things inside.

Below: **Mrs. Astor's sitting room is decorated in the English country house tradition, with lots of chintz and a needlepoint footstool and pillows bearing dog motifs. The smaller of the two full-length studies of women on the wall is a portrait of Mrs. Astor by Cecil Beaton.** *Opposite:* **A 17th-century portrait of a working dog of that era, by Dutch painter Ferdinand Bol, takes center stage in the formal living room; the boat scene to the right was painted by Raoul Dufy.**

Clockwise from top left: **The carved wood box with a pack of dogs on it, among English and Chinese ceramic dog figures, was a gift from Pamela Harriman; a sign at the entrance to Holly Hill; a pawprint fabric chair, drawings of dogs, and treasured personal souvenirs are found in a room adjacent to the entry hall; a porcelain box, for storing collars for small dogs, forms part of the canine tablescape.** Right: **Of the scores of English and American dog paintings in the entry hall, some were acquired by Mrs. Astor decades ago; others are more recent gifts from friends.**

Above, left to right: **Dog paintings, including one by Sir Edwin Landseer (second from bottom on left); an antique majolica tureen; Brooke Astor's writing desk, covered with memorabilia, including a favorite photograph of Vincent Astor.**
Below: **Holly Hill, where Mrs. Astor spends weekends from the fall through spring every year, enjoys a sweeping view of the Hudson River from its upper stories.**

Of the material objects she has accumulated over nine decades, Brooke Astor wrote, in her autobiography *Footprints,* "They are my friends and I cannot throw them out just because they have become outdated and shabby." Now she extracts a miniature pair of bejeweled spectacles from the drawer and carefully places them on the nose of a carved hound snuffbox on the console. "I used to do that to have a bit of fun," she chirps, then replaces the spectacles and produces a tiny tin cowboy hat. She stares at it for a long moment, then turns to her visitor and says, "Would you like to have this?"

Although the object has no particular value, the visitor hesitates. But the philanthropist insists, pressing it into his hand. The visitor is strangely moved by this odd act of generosity.

Just then, Boysie and Girlsie come skittering across the marble floor. At once they are gathered up and brought to the car. (A third dog, Maizie, a fifteen-year-old schnauzer, is not well enough to travel.) The dachshunds settle into the backseat, on a towel, and immediately close their eyes. After saying her good-byes, Mrs. Astor exits through the door. A petite woman, she all but vanishes once she sits down in the car next to the dogs. The Lincoln moves slowly away, taking New York's "guardian angel" home.

PART FOUR

Dogs
at
REST

❖ ◆ ● ● ❖

"Old Blue died and he died so hard, shook the ground in my backyard," wrote the anonymous author whose poem begins *Dog Music*, a unique anthology of more than 160 poems about dogs written in the 20th century, virtually all of them by American poets. While the tone of the largely celebratory volume ranges wildly, from comic to contemplative, a surprising number of the poems, directly or indirectly, touch on the demise of a favorite dog. From "Elegy for a Beagle Mutt," by

Liz Rosenberg, to "Dog's Death," by John Updike, a master of small-animal death scenes, these poems capture the special character of a certain dog and explore the emotions associated with its loss.

Such poems, in fact, are a form of catharsis, or closure, for people who have loved their dogs and lost them, and, increasingly, that need for emotional release has become a paramount concern among the dog-owning population. This is partly because dog owners relate to their dogs more personally than ever before, and partly because more dog owners—as many as 15 percent of the total U.S. population—are one-person households for whom their dog is the main source of companionship.

As for catharsis, the bad news is that most dog owners are unable to expiate their grief through poetry—at least of the kind that is publishable. But the good news is that there are now many other avenues for getting through the loss of a pet. In fact, probably more than any other social, economic, or cultural evidence of the importance of dogs in society, the rise in such services as grief-counseling hot lines at humane societies and veterinary hospitals across the country proves the depth and power of the canine connection.

These grief counselors say it is good and proper to weep for our dogs in death, just as it was incumbent on us to sing their praises in life, even though our words usually fell on deaf ears. The gaping discrepancy in the life expectancies of *Homo sapiens* and *Canis familiaris* means that most people who love dogs are destined to outlive the puppies they bring home. In spite of that hard fact, most dog owners do not give up on dogs after losing their first one. Rather, usually after a decent interval, they get another one, and then, after another loss, yet another one, and this process goes on more or less indefinitely. Dogs span out years through thick and thin, in sickness and in health, from one job to the next, in zip code after zip code, until finally we are the ones that death doth part, at which point, we hope, our last dog of choice has the courtesy to pull a long face.

Pet owners used to just bury their dear departed in the backyard, and in some ways the ritual of burial still provides the ultimate expression of farewell.

The nation's oldest canine graveyard, Hartsdale Pet Cemetery, got started in 1896 when a New York City veterinarian, Dr. Samuel Johnson, offered his apple orchard in then rural Westchester County to serve as a burial plot for the dog of a friend who was much bereaved. There are now some 70,000 graves in this cemetery. Many of the early monuments found here are as artfully produced as those found in human cemeteries, such as the granite doghouse dedicated to Buster and Queenie in the 1940s, or the massive dark rock outcropping with the single name, Rex, carved in its side.

Hartsdale is one of hundreds of pet cemeteries in the United States, some small, some large, some up to date on the art of canine undertaking, others lost in time.

Bubbling Well Pet Memorial Park in Napa, California, covering 20 acres of green hills and tended gardens, was built on a dump site in the 1960s and features a petting zoo with pygmy goats, emus, and llamas. One patron has buried four generations of Chihuahuas here. "It's like a serene park where people can come during their sadness for some peace of mind and remember some of the positives of their pets," reports *Dog Fancy* magazine.

Aspin Hill Memorial Park in suburban Maryland, by contrast, has the weather-

Above and opposite: **Hartsdale Pet Cemetery, established in 1896, offers tributes to beloved dogs, some as stolid as a dachshund sculpture, others as poignant as favorite photographs of the deceased.**

IN LOVING MEMORY
OF
ROBERT BURNS
JULY 10, 1916,
APRIL 4, 1921.
———
JOHN S. THACHER JR.

OUR PRECIOUS PETS

"DAISY"
915 — 1932

"BOOTS"
1932

This page and opposite: **While religious themes crop up from time to time on canine headstones, most people who bury a dog in a pet cemetery send off the creature with a simple epitaph honoring its earthly existence.**
Following pages: **The War Dog Memorial in Harstdale Pet Cemetery, a 10-foot-high monument to the dogs that served in World War I, was erected in 1923 through public contributions.**

DEDICATED
TO THE MEMORY OF
THE WAR DO
ERECTED BY PUBLIC CONTRI
BY DOG LOVERS, TO MAN'S
FAITHFUL FRIEND. FOR THE V
SERVICES RENDERED IN
WORLD WA
1914 — 1918

stained and pockmarked stone tablets and figures of another time and place, some dating from before the 1920s—ghosts of dogs near the extinction of human memory. "Part of my heart is buried here," reads the epitaph for Sonny Boy, a cocker spaniel, shown in full stride carrying a rolled-up newspaper, in a photograph encased in the tablet. Another stone shows a wire-haired terrier named Luckie, sitting up jauntily with a corncob pipe in his mouth.

"Some people think it's crazy to have a place to bury pets, and even some of the people who come here feel foolish," observes Edward Martin Jr., co-owner of Hartsdale Pet Cemetery, who has known the place since he was a child—his father engraved many of the headstones found here. "But they shouldn't. They're not odd people. They're caring people who wanted to do right by the pets they loved." The best thing that James Thurber could say about an Airedale named Muggs, one of numerous dogs he owned over a lifetime, was that "he never bit anyone more than once at a time."

Yet even Muggs deserved to be dispatched with a modicum of respect when his time came, as Thurber related:

Mother wanted to bury him in the family plot under a marble stone with some such inscription as "Flights of angels sing thee to thy rest!" but we persuaded her it was against the law. In the end we just put up a smooth board above his grave along a lonely road. On the board I wrote with an indelible pencil, "Cave Canem." Mother was quite pleased with the simple classic dignity of the old Latin epitaph.

Opposite and below: **So strong is the connection that humans feel to their dogs that it is not unusual for owners to bestow their own last names on departed canines.**

BRADLEAH COCKERS

DEAR LORD, PROTECT AND BLESS
THY BEASTS AND SINGING BIRDS
AND GUARD, WITH TENDERNESS
SMALL ONES, WHO HAVE NO WORDS

Above and opposite: **On an evening in early spring, before it has received its first mowing of the season, Aspin Hill Memorial Park radiates the mystery of the unforgotten.** *Below:* **Breed-specific headstones, like photographs, help to preserve an identity for the dog one has lost.**

Directory for Dog Lovers

MUSEUMS AND LIBRARIES

American Kennel Club Library

260 Madison Ave.
New York, NY 10016
(212) 696-8200
Some 15,000 volumes covering more than 200 purebred dogs and a host of other canine topics; a small collection of fine 19th-century and early-20th-century art also on exhibit.

The Dog Museum

1721 South Mason Rd.
St. Louis, MO 63131
(314) 821-DOGS
Vast collection, housed in a historic residence in scenic Queeny Park, includes paintings, drawings, photographs, sculptures, artifacts, ceramics, books, and videos.

Fire Museum

1301 York Rd.
Lutherville, MD 21093
(410) 321-7500
Art and artifacts document role of the Dalmatian in history of firefighting.

Opposite: **Antique snuffboxes and walking sticks, fashioned after favorite breeds, are prized collectibles of dogs lovers.**

Morven Park

17263 Southern Planter La.
P.O. Box 6228
Leesburg, VA 20178
(703) 777-2414
Collection of paintings, bronzes, photos portraying famous hounds, huntsmen, and hunts in North America and England; also beagling artifacts. Site of all-breed dog show and Virginia Foxhound Club hound show every spring.

National Bird Dog Museum

P.O. Box 544
Grand Junction, TN 38039
(901) 764-2058
Art, artifacts, literature, photography, and other memorabilia gathered to preserve the history of bird hunting with some 36 distinct breeds of pointing dogs, spaniels, and retrievers.

Pebble Hill Plantation

P.O. Box 830
U.S. Highway 319
Thomasville, GA 31799
(912) 226-2344
Museum houses the extensive sporting art collection of Elisabeth Ireland "Miss Pansy" Poe; also stables, kennels, dog hospital, and horse and dog cemetery.

GALLERIES

Animal Art Antiques
617 Chartres St.
New Orleans, LA
(504) 529-4407
animalart@email.msn.com
Paintings, furniture, silver, porcelain, majolica, and many other items in a shop dedicated to things with an animal motif.

Ian Peck Fine Paintings
980 Madison Ave.
New York, NY 10021
(212) 396-2442
Fax 212-396-2444
ianpeck@sprynet.com
Fine horse and dog paintings.

Red Fox Fine Art
9 North Liberty St.
Middleburg, VA 20117
(540) 687-5780
Fax 540-687-3338
fineart@redfox.com
Fine 19th-century animal and sporting paintings and bronze sculptures.

William Secord Gallery, Inc.
52 East 76th St.
New York, NY 10021
(212) 249-0075
Fax 212-288-1938
wsecord@dogpainting.com
Wide range of 19th- and early-20th-century dog paintings, including British and American masters of the genre such as Maud Earl and John Emms as well as contemporary artists Christine Merrill, Joseph H. Sulkowski, and Barrie Barnett.

DEALERS IN ANTIQUES, BOOKS, AND COLLECTIBLES
(most by appointment only)

A to Z Collectibles
Maryann Allums and Nancy Zogg
Lovers Lane Antiques Market
5001 West Lovers La.
Dallas, TX
(214) 351-5656
Vintage dog paintings, prints, and decorative objects.

All Dogs
Gail McDonald
766 Willard St. A-10
Quincy, MA 02169
(781) 871-5380
woofies1@webtv.net
In addition to more 8,000 books, a variety of canine art and artifacts.

American Sampler
Nancy and John C. Smith
Box 371
Barnesville, MD 20838
(301) 972-6250
Painted cast-iron dog doorstops and bookends.

Bibliography of the Dog
Nigel Aubrey-Jones
P.O. Box 118
Churubusco, NY 12923
(514) 826-0711
One of the most respected dealers in rare and out-of-print dog books in the United States.

The Bowsery
Carolee Jortner
34360 Highway 101 South
P.O. Box 146
Cloverdale, OR 97112-0146
(503) 392-4499
Dog-related antiques, art objects, and collectibles.

Bryan's Books
Bryan Cummins
67 Downey Dr.
Bolton, Ontario
Canada L7E2B8
(905) 857-9370
loreby@pathcom.com
Rare, antiquarian, and out-of-print dog books.

Carol Butcher Books
3955 New Rd.
Youngstown, OH 44515
(330) 793-6832
Rare and out-of-print dog books.

Clifford Hubbard's Bookshop
Ffynnon Cado, Ponterwyd
Aberystwyth, Ceredigion
Wales SY23
United Kingdom
Active in the rare-book trade for decades, the legendary "Doggie" Hubbard is considered the dean of dog books.

Dog Lovers Bookshop
Margot Rosenberg & Bern Marcowitz
9 West 31st St. (2nd Floor)
New York, NY 10001
(212) 594-3601
Wide variety of canine books, including out-of-print titles, and dog-related gifts.

Dog Ink
Kathy Darling
46 Cooper La.
Larchmont, NY 10538
(914) 834-9029
Canine art and artifacts, with books a special emphasis.

Doggone Books and Collectibles
Joanne & Craig Francisco
2215 Motor Parkway
Ronkonkoma, NY 11779
(516) 981-5057
CRAJO1970@aol.com
Anything of quality related to the dog, from books to pictures and porcelains; no reproductions. (Craig Francisco is also a professional dog trainer.)

The Dog Lady
Jo Ellen Arnold
P.O. Box 2641
Springfield, VA 22152
(703) 644-5202
Fine canine collectibles including porcelains, bronzes, and paintings.

4-M Enterprises
Viola Neal
1280 Pacific St.
Union City, CA 94587
(800) 487-9867
New and out-of-print dog books and videos. Catalog.

Fred Cesana
49 East Main St.
Plainville, CT 06062
(860) 747-2759
Antique veterinary patent medicines and memorabilia including early-20th-century advertising signs, posters, and cabinets.

Henniker Kennel Company Antiques
Nancy A. Bergendahl
2 Old Ireland Rd.
Henniker, NH 03242
(603) 428-7136
nbergendahl@conknet.com
Antique and collectible canines in all forms.

June Ainsworth
P.O. Box 2212
East Hampton, NY 11937
(516) 324-2296
Dog paintings, pottery, and other decorative objects.

Kanine Collectibles
247 Christian Ave.
Box 271
Stony Brook, NY 11790
(516) 751-2805

King Llewellin Setters
Alfred and Drenda King
P.O. Drawer 100
Enola, AR 72047
(501) 336-8510
Specializing in English setters.

Purple Shamrock
Darcy Bannigan
P.O. Box 3595
Springfield, MO 65808
(417) 882-7777
Antique and new dog art pieces including ones of hard-to-find breeds, original and limited-edition contemporary bronzes, porcelains from England and Germany.

The Retriever Antiques
Ticia Robak
P.O. Box 12
Yarmouth Port, MA 02675
(508) 362-3096
www.theretriever.com
Dog-related items made before 1950.

Tarmans Books
Mary Ellen Tarman
28 West Main St.
Hummelstown, PA 17036
(717) 566-7030
Fax 717-566-9843
tarmans@ezonline.com
Shop with more than 20,000 out-of-print books including canine titles.

Tigger's Dog Stuff
Meg W. Weitz and Michael Greenberg
601 Rockwood Rd.
Wilmington, DE 19802
(302) 762-8939
DOG4HIRE@aol.com
*Broad assortment of canine materials, including books,
paintings, porcelains, bronzes, pottery pieces, jewelry,
and postcards.*

Time-N-Type Books
Harold and Sylvia Howison
5122 Vines Rd.
Howell, MI 48843
(734) 878-9417
Out-of-print dog books.

R.E. and G.B. Way, A.B.A.
Brettons, Burrough Green
Newmarket
Suffolk, CB8 9NA
England
01638 507217
Antiquarian dog books.

PAINTERS, PHOTOGRAPHERS, SCULPTORS, AND CRAFTS

Animal Manors
462 West 23rd St., Suite 1
New York, NY 10011
(212) 206-6231
Custom-built dog houses.

Christine Merrill
c/o William Secord Gallery
52 East 76th St.
New York, NY 10021
(212) 249-0075
*Oil portraits in the classic 18th-century style of animal
portraiture.*

Countryhouse Studios
RD 2
Annville, PA 17003
(717) 867-2135
Dog photography.

Dan & Dee Bates
BrookHaven
32 Old Wilson La.
Route 1, Box 342
High View, WV 26808
(304) 856-2972
Original animal sculptures in bronze and cold-cast bronze.

Joseph H. Sulkowsi
c/o William Secord Gallery
52 East 76th St.
New York, NY 10021
Oil portraits on canvas or panel.

Jane Millett
10 Downing St.
Apt. 1R
New York, NY 10014
(212) 924-6263
Dog paintings.

Julie Evans
203 West 85th St.
Apt. 52
New York, NY 10024
(212) 496-9007
Miniature dog portraits.

Lime Rock Gallery
100 West Main St.
P.O. Box 340
Sackets Harbor, NY 13685
(315) 646-3000
Sporting dog bronzes by the gallery's owner, Robert Wehle.

McAdoo Rugs
1 Pleasant St.
P.O. Box 847
North Bennington, VT 05257
(802) 442-3563
www.mcadoorugs.com
Hooked rugs in standard and custom designs, including dog motifs, made from New Zealand wool spun into rug yarn in Philadelphia and hand-dyed.

Petography
25 Central Park West
New York, NY
(800) 738-6472
Classic animal portraiture by photographer Jim Dratfield.

Photography by Randy
Randy Handwerger
8 Folkstone Dr.
East Hampton, NY 11937
(516) 324-3904
Pet photography.

Valerie Shaff
c/o Bridgewater/Lustberg Gallery
560 Broadway, Suite 204
New York, NY
(212) 941-6355
Portrait photography of dogs.

Stephen Huneck Gallery
49 Central St.
P.O. Box 59
Woodstock, VT 05091
(800) 449-2580
Gallery exhibits owner Stephen Huneck's folk-style prints and sculptures of dogs as well as lamps and furniture incorporating dog imagery.

Walter T. Matia
Curlew Castings
18601 Darnestown Rd.
Poolesville, MD 20837
(301) 349-2330
Original animal sculptures in bronze.

Wooden It Be Lovely
Herb Morgan Designs
1486 Sheffield Dr. NE
Atlanta, GA 30329-3422
(404) 325-4701
Custom plant stands, tables, and other whimsical creations in the shape of dogs.

PERIODICALS AND NEWSLETTERS

AKC Gazette
5580 Centerview Dr.
Raleigh, NC 27690-0643
Monthly journal of the American Kennel Club.

Canine Collectibles Quarterly
10290 Hill Rd.
Erie, IL 61250
(309) 659-2166
Features and reports on dog antiques and collectibles.

Canine Images
1003 Central Ave.
Fort Dodge, IA 50501
(515) 955-1600
Published three times a year, with focus on fine art and furnishings for the dog lover.

DGNY
981 First Ave., Suite 140
New York, NY 10022
(212) 832-2828
Bimonthly guide to owning a dog in New York City.

Dog Fancy
P.O. Box 6050
Mission Viejo, CA 92690
(714) 855-8822
Monthly magazine for dog lovers.

DogGone
P.O. Box 65155
Vero Beach, FL 32965-1155
(407) 569-8434
Bimonthly newsletter with tips for traveling with dogs and information on places that allow dogs to stay on the premises.

BOUTIQUES AND BAKERIES

Angel Dog
131 Charles St.
Beacon Hill
Boston, MA 02114
(617) 742-6435
*Clocks, ceramics, china, sculptures, jewelry, needlepoint
pillows, letter openers, weather vanes, bells, collars, men's
suspenders and ties, and other gift items carrying motifs
of more than 300 breeds.*

Three Dog Bakery
612 West 48th St.
Kansas City, MO
(816) 474-3647
Various canine dog biscuits and soft-baked items.

The Barkery
Hank and Arlene Macellaro
3330 West 26th St.
Erie, PA 16506
(800) 965-0455
*Dog treats from all-natural ingredients, including cheese-
burger biscuits, sirloin shakes, and pup-a-roni pizzas.*

DogWatch
Cornell University College of Veterinary Medicine
P.O. Box 420235
Palm Coast, FL 32142-0235
*Monthly newsletter on care and feeding of dogs, with
information on specific breeds and behavior.*

Veterinary Collectible Roundtable
7431 Covington Highway
Lithonia, GA 30058
(770) 482-5100
*Newsletter dedicated to antique veterinary patent medicines
and related collectibles.*

Your Dog
Tufts University School of Veterinary Medicine
200 Westboro Rd.
North Grafton, MA 01536
*Monthly newsletter devoted to canine medical and behav-
ioral information.*

Le Chien Trump Plaza
1044 Third Ave.
New York, NY
(212) 861-8100
*Dog clothing, accessories, canine perfume, and grooming,
with holistic bath, massage, and clipping.*

Not Just Dogs
244 East 60th St.
New York, NY
(212) 752-8669
*High-end dog clothing and accessories, including leashes,
collars, coats, and beds.*

Doggie Do and Pussy Cats, Too
567 Third Ave.
New York, NY
(212) 661-9111
*Dog clothing and accessories, including silver dog statues
and painted banquet tables with metal bowls and custom dog
portraits.*

Canine Styles
830 Lexington Ave.
New York, NY 10021
(212) 751-4549
Dog grooming and accessories, including St. Moritz collars and leashes from Switzerland, Burberry dog coats, custom-made dog beds.

All Greatures Great and Small
833 Lexington Ave.
New York, NY 10021
(212) 754-MEOW
Gifts and supplies for pets and pet owners.

CATALOGS

George
2411 California at Fillmore
San Francisco, CA 94115
(415) 922-9111
Jackets, slickers, crewneck and turtleneck sweaters, beds and quilts, bowls and bandannas, collars and leads, and more.

The Black Duck
Box 2219
Vineyard Haven, MA 02568
(800) 626-1991
Flavored dog treats, leads and collars, T-shirts, boxer shorts, sweatshirts, and restaurantware.

In the Company of Dogs
P.O. Box 7071
Dover, DE 19903
(800) 924-5050
Items include futons, damask beds, personalized picture frames, peg racks, collage watches and photo pillows, decoupage frames and trays, and hand-hooked rugs.

CAMPS/TRAINING SCHOOLS

Camp Winnaribbun
High Rollers Obedience Association
P.O. Box 50300
Reno, NV 89513
(702) 747-1561
Tracking, agility, flyball, and obedience are among the activities offered on a secluded 32-acre pine forest with private beach; also, clinics on homeopathy and hands-on healing techniques for the ailing dog.

Camp Gone to the Dogs
Honey Loring, Director
RR 1, Box 958
Putney, VT 05346
(802) 387-5673
Weekend and weeklong camp sessions offer wide range of activities for dogs and their owners, including swimming, tracking, lure coursing, agility and obedience trials; evening talks on various dog-related topics.

Manhattan Dog Training & Behavior Center
145 West 18th St.
New York, NY 10011
(212) 213-4288
Puppy kindergarten, group classes, private tutorials, overnights.

Triple Crown Dog Academy
200 County Rd. 197
Hutto, TX 78634
(512) 759-2275
Training facility on 350 acres, near Austin, with ponds for swimming, fields for tracking, spacious kennels, and a 32,000-square-foot arena equipped with high-traction, shock-absorbing flooring.

COUNTRY HOTELS

Twin Farms
Shaun and Beverley Matthews, managing directors
Barnard, VT 05031
(802) 234-9999

PET CEMETERIES

Hartsdale Pet Cemetery
75 North Central Park Ave.
Hartsdale, NY 10530
(800) 375-5234

Accredited Pet Cemeteries Society
139 West Rush Rd.
West Rush, NY 14543
(716) 533-1685

International Association of Pet Cemeteries
Route 11, Box 163
Ellensburg Depot, NY 12935
(518) 594-300

Acknowledgments

We would like to express our gratitude to all the dog owners and dog lovers who were kind enough to let us into their houses, apartments, studios, clubs, offices, kennels—into their very lives—in order for us to compile this rich assortment of canine images and experiences. Although we can't possibly mention all the people who lent a hand along the way, we would be remiss not to single out the individuals without whom the book certainly could not have gone forward, including Bill Secord, of William Secord Gallery, for his guidance and enthusiasm from day one; Jo-Ann Brown, also of William Secord Gallery; Cathy and John Nelson; Bob and Gatra Whele of Elhew Kennels, for their kindness and hospitality; Tom Bradley of the Westminster Kennel Club; Philip Crawford, for sharing his vast Abercrombie & Fitch collection; Barbara Kolk and Jeanine O'Kane of the American Kennel Club; Cindy Lang and her springer spaniels, along with Barbara and Cary Haupt, Sarah Aley, Greg and Nadine Mort and their children, also Laura Sprague,

Susanna Srague, and Annie Bailey, Ted Bean, and Jack Baker, all of Maine's beautiful Saint George peninsula; Shaun and Beverley Matthews, the perfect hosts at Twin Farms, Barnard, Vermont; Nancy Bergendahl, Patricia Robak, and Jo Ellen Arnold, ardent collectors and dealers who passed along many valuable leads to us; Lisa Gilford of Le Chien and Cynthia and Christopher DesBrisay of Angel Dog; Dave and Ruth Morine, for putting us up, and putting up with us, in Virginia; Linda Cowasjee and her Windermere Farm Jack Russell terriers; Miranda Kettlewell and Stephen Sloan; Walt Matia, sculptor, sportsman, and cook; the nonpareil collector of dog books, Mr. F. P. Fretwell; Brenda Buckles of the French Bull Dog Club of America; Marty Ross, old friend and trusty resource; Miss Daphne Hereford, German shepherd breeder and president of Rin Tin Tin, Inc.; Elouise Cooper and Marthann Weaber, stalwart supporters and morale builders throughout the project; Dr. Marston Jones, eminent Chesapeake Bay retriever trainer and breeder, and Bobby Burris of Pintail Point; Polly and Donald Bruckmann and their brood of Shelties; Christine Merrill and Valerie Shaff, who specialize in making dogs immortal in their chosen art forms; Virginia Keresey and Brennan Pelosi, for their untiring assistance under trying circumstances; Boston interior designer Betsy Speert; Honey Loring and her exuberant staff at Camp Gone to the Dogs; Nat Day, president of The Leash, and his board, for kindly letting us photograph his unique club's sublime tributes to the dog in many forms; Shirlee and Larry Kalstone, for sharing their exquisite collection of canine walking sticks; the Montgomery County Kennel Club; the Working Australian Shepherd Club of Upstate New York; Toni Lake and the Australian Shepherd Club of New England; Carolyne Roehm and her helpful staff at Weatherstone; Dr. Fred Cesana, with particular thanks for introducing us to the roving English setter, Buster; Peter Winants of the National Sporting Library; horse and dog lover Melanie Fleischmann; Mrs. John B. Hannum and her huntsman, Joe Cassidy of Mr. Stewart's Cheshire Foxhounds; Edgar Gould and his well-schooled border collies; the venerable Virginia Foxhound Club; Mrs. Brooke Astor and the staff at Holly Hill, including Christopher Ely, Carmine Fasciani, and Jolee Hirsch.

Once again, we are grateful to our agents, Gayle Benderoff and Deborah Geltman, for their labors in our behalf and especially for their wit and their pep talks. For saving our neck, editorially, we thank Lauren Shakely, Kathryn Crosby, and Mark McCauslin. And for making this book graphically Best in Show, we give special thanks to MarySarah Quinn, who liked our book from the start; Maggie Hinders, who handled our second-guessing with aplomb; Joy Sikorski, who took care of the production details; and, especially, designer Donna Agajanian, for her vision.

Index